京城胡同留真
LIFE IN HUTONGS
*Through Intricate
Alleyways in Beijing*

Shen Yantai
Wang Changqing
沈延太　王长青

京城胡同留真
LIFE IN HUTONGS
Through Intricate Alleyways in Beijing

外文出版社　北京
FOREIGN LANGUAGES PRESS　BEIJING

1997年第一版

责任编辑： 廖 频
装帧设计： 蔡 荣

First Edition   1997

Text by Shen Yantai
Photos by Shen Yantai and Wang Changqing
Translated by Huang Youyi
Edited by Liao Pin
Designed by Cai Rong

ISBN 7-119-01917-1
© Foreign Languages Press   1997
Published by Foreign Languages Press
24 Baiwanzhuang Road, Beijing, 100037, China
Printed by Shenzhen Donnelley Bright Sun Printing Co. Ltd.
Distributed by China International Book Trading Corporation
19 Chegongzhuang Road, Beijing, 100044, China
Printed in People's Republic of China

Contents

Preface   6
Alleys and lanes around the Forbidden City   10
The physical history of the alleys and lanes   28
Quadrangle houses in the alleys and lanes   90
Life in the alleys and lanes   136
Changes in the alleys and lanes   180
Afterword   188

目 录

序言   6
紫禁城下的胡同   10
胡同景观   28
胡同里的四合院   90
胡同风情   136
胡同的变迁   180
后记   188

Preface

by *Liang Bingkun**

Born and bred in Beijing and having spent more than a half century of my life here, I probably qualify to be a "real old Beijinger".

What is most unforgettable in Beijing? It is the many long and short, wide and narrow alleys and lanes. Whenever I go on a trip away from home, particularly on a trip abroad, what I miss most are the ancient, elegant, familiar, lovable and plain lanes. In other words, unless I am back in the lanes, I have not returned home. Home is inseparable from the alleys and lanes. Nor is Beijing separable from them. To a certain extent, the alleys and lanes are the soul of Beijing.

Then just how many alleys and lanes are there in Beijing? Veteran residents say: "The major ones number 360 and small ones are as many as hairs on an ox." Men of letters have used the term of several thousand to describe the lanes. According to incomplete statistics, by 1949, there had been a total of over 6,000 lanes within the boundary of Beijing, out of which over 4,550 were located in the inner city districts. Naturally, the figure for today is much more impressive than that.

In my view, the term "culture" probably refers to a particular way of life. People of different times have different ways of life and thus live in different cultures. In this sense, for generations, people in Beijing have lived in a culture of lanes. As time goes by, especially with the progress of urban construction, lanes in Beijing are decreasing in number. On their ground, tall buildings are springing up. It is against this background, Shen Yantai and Wang Changqing, the couple photographers, have presented readers with this collection of *Through the Intricate Alleyways in Beijing*. Just as they state it in the "Afterword" of this work, they were not prepared "for the sudden disappearing of the lanes which have presented a culture of a particular historic time. We feel it an urgent task to capture the sights and sounds through the camera lens, recording the historic footprints of the culture of lanes in this ancient capital city, the myriad vistas of people, their typical ways of life and customs and habits unique to these lanes. Our contribution may not amount to much of a creative surprise. It was meant an attempt to rescue a cultural heritage, collecting data of images for people to do research and studies of a passing culture in the future. We found this a worthwhile job, though it was hard and cost a lot of time and sweat. In doing so, we were not going after monetary payment, or an award of any kind, but simply driven by a sense of duty." Reading these words, shouldn't we cheer them for their rescue operation?

Having read the book, I was profoundly moved by "fiery" passions that are present throughout the work.

First, the passion of the photographers.

Interestingly, neither of the couple is a native of Beijing, as he was born in Shanghai in the south and she in Taiyuan, Shanxi, west of Beijing. But they all have lived for many years in Beijing and more importantly cherish a deep love of the city. They have a particular sentiment for the alleys and lanes here and their hearts beat to the rhythm of life in the alleys and lanes. To a certain extent, the lanes have become part of their life. As a result, when they focus their camera on the lanes, their own passion goes into their work, thus arousing a strong response from whoever sees their work. When I looked at their photos, I could not help thinking that what I was actually seeing was the abstract but ubiquitous souls of the photographers rather than the concrete images in the photographs. I believe this passion and sentiment are the most valuable and irreplaceable qualities of an artist, which renders the works with a strong vitality.

Second, the passion and sentiment in the works.

It can be said that every picture in the book, with or without people in it, whether taken in the spring sunshine, summer rain, autumn wind or winter snow, focuses on the people and thus on the sentiment in the alleyways. I want to particularly point out that the photographers have displayed a boundless love and longing for the alleys and lanes in Beijing through their pictures. They told this encounter. One day they walked in an old quadrangle house which was being torn down and saw an elderly man standing in front of broken walls. His entirely family had moved into a new apartment building, but he was reluctant to part with the soon-to-disappear dwellings, where perhaps he had spent his life of childhood, youth, middle-age and part of his senior years. He looked as if he wanted to cry, but managed to hold back his tears. He wanted to say something but words failed him. His last act was to pick and take away with him the last ripen Chinese wolfberry fruit. Perhaps it was this discovery with a shattering impact that gave them the inspiration for the picture entitled "Difficult to part with the old house". In this photo, an old man stood in front of a broken wall in a deadly quiet surrounding. He stared at what was in front of him with a helpless expression on the face. His mouth seemed to be moving but no words came out.... Works like this lead readers to vividly feel that the old man seems to just have had a heart-to-heart and moving conversation with the photographers. I remember the great writer Tolstoy once said that the impact of art was determined by three elements in the work and two of them being "the unique characteristics of the sentiment it conveys" and "the explicitness of such sentiment it conveys". The artistic impact of this photo is so enormous and profound that readers will find it hard to forget.

Finally, let me congratulate the publication of *Through the Intricate Alleyways in Beijing*. I look forward to seeing more, newer and better works from the two author-photographers.

In photography, I am a layman. What I have written is therefore an observation of an ordinary reader.

I thank the authors and the readers.

Summer 1996, Beijing

---

*Liang Bingkun is a playwright with Beijing People's Art Theater and holds the academic title of a first-class writer. He is a member of both the China Writers Association and China Playwrights Association.

序 言

梁秉堃

笔者生在北京,长在北京,半个多世纪过去了,大约算得上是个地道的"老北京"。北京城里最使人难以忘怀是什么呢?就是那大大小小的、在南方被叫做街巷的胡同。每当我从外地特别是从外国出差归来的时候,最急于想见到的便是那一条条古朴的、幽雅的、熟悉的、亲切的胡同。或者说,只有见到了这些胡同才能算是回到了北京,回到了家。胡同与家分不开,北京与胡同分不开。一定意义上说,胡同就是北京的魂。

据说,"胡同"一词出现在金、元时代,来源于蒙古语系,是女真人和蒙古人进入中原以后,按照自己的习惯把城市的街巷称为"胡同"的。那么,北京到底有多少胡同呢?听老人们说:"大胡同三百六,小胡同如牛毛。"意思是,多得数也数不清。为此,文人们也有"庶五城胡同,浩繁几千条之间"一说。根据不完全的统计,北京全城到1949年为止,已经有胡同6000多条,城区里的胡同有4550多条。自然,现在又要比这个数字大得多了。到底有多少,似乎谁也说不清。

我以为,所谓"文化",大约就是人们的一种生活方式,不同的时代人们有着不同的生活方式,也就有着不同的文化。或许从这个角度来看,北京人正是祖祖辈辈生活在"胡同文化"里的。随着时代的发展,特别是随着城市建设的发展,北京城的胡同越来越少,代之为一栋栋高楼大厦。正是在这种情况下,沈延太、王长青两位摄影家把这本《京城胡同留真》画册奉献给广大读者。正如他们在"后记"中所言:"我们深为胡同作为一个特定历史时代的文化的不辞而别而感到措手不及,胡同文化的面貌急待用摄影纪实的手法'留真'下来。尽我们微薄的力量留下一些古都胡同文化的历史陈迹,胡同天地里的百姓世相,京味京韵的民俗风情和市井氛围,虽算不上惊人的创作,却干了一点抢救遗产的活儿,为后来者追寻、研究即将逝去的胡同文化,留一点形象的资料。这是摄影力所能及的一种功能,作为从事摄影的苦力,流点汗也是值得的,不求报酬,不图奖赏,责任感的驱使,仅此而已。"读到这里,难道我们还不应该为他们的"抢救",为他们的"留真"拍手叫好,倍加称赞吗?

我看过画册以后,深深地被一个像火一样燃烧着的"情"字所吸引,所打动,所感染。

首先说作者的情。

说来也巧,两位摄影家都不是土著的北京人,一位生于江南的上海,一位生于山西的太原。然而,他们都久居北京,更重要的是热爱北京,他们对北京城的胡同情有独钟,息息相关,一定意义上说,胡同已经成了他们生命的一部分。因此,他们在用手中照相机进行纪实留真的时候,就不能不融进了自己沉甸甸的情感,从而使读者也得到强烈的共鸣。在欣赏作品的时候我就想,与其说是看到了照片上的具体形象,不如说是看到了作者那抽象的又无所不在的灵魂。我以为,这些也许是一个艺术创作者最可宝贵的东西,不可代替的东西,使作品能够富有强大生命力的东西。

其次说作品的情。

可以说,这里的每一幅作品,不管是有人物出现的,没人物出现的,也不管是在春光里、夏雨里、秋风里、冬雪里,作者始终把镜头对准了胡同里的人。因而,也就把镜头对准了情。我想特别要指出的是,作者通过作品表现出一种对于京城胡同的无限眷恋之情。作者讲了这样一件事——有一天,他们走进了一片正在拆迁的四合院老房子之间,看见在已经拆毁的断墙残壁前站着一位老人,他的全家已经搬进新建的公寓楼房,可他还是恋恋不舍地来看看这些行将消失的老房子,也许他就是在这座老房子里生老房子里长的,老房子里留下了他的童年,他的青年,他的中年,和他的一部分老年,他欲言又止,欲哭无泪,最后摘走了老院子里最后一束红透的枸杞子。大约正是这个具有震撼力的形象发现,使得他们创作了《故宅难舍》那幅照片。那里也有一位老人,也是站在已经拆毁的断墙残壁跟前,周围安静得没有一点声音,他双目凝视着眼前的一切,脸上呈现出有些茫然的表情,蠕动的嘴里仿佛有着说不出又说不尽的话⋯⋯这些使读者真切地感觉到,老人似乎是刚刚和作者进行过一次推心置腹地,又激动万分的谈话。记得,大作家托尔斯泰说过,艺术感染力大小、深浅,取决于作品表现出的三个要素,其中的两个便是"所传达的感情具有多么大的独特性"和"这种感情的传达有多么清晰"。应当说,这幅照片的艺术感染力是大的,是深的,是使读者容易记住又不忍心忘掉的。

最后,我要衷心地祝贺《京城胡同留真》的出版,并企盼将来能够看到两位作者更新、更好、更多的作品问世。

对于摄影艺术我是个外行,说不出什么精彩的意见来,写在这里的只不过是一个普通读者的观后感而已。

谢谢作者,也谢谢读者。

1996年夏日于京城

梁秉堃　国家一级作家、北京人民艺术剧院编剧,为中国作家协会和中国戏剧家协会会员。

Alleys and lanes around the Forbidden City

Half a century ago, the Forbidden City and its surrounding lanes constituted the two major component parts of the city of Beijing. The former housed the living quarters of dynastic rulers and their families, and the latter was home to ordinary citizens, dotted now and then by palace-like residences of past princes and dukes.

A town within a town, the Forbidden City was located right in the center of Beijing. From its completion in 1420 till 1911 when the last emperor in China was forced to abdicate, it served as the sacred ground for the rulers and their family members. Today, it is called the Palace Museum, open to the public. Its solid, high and thick walls and deep and wide moat on all four sides once made it an impregnable bastion. To strengthen its defense, additional walls were also built to form a defense city called the Royal City outside the palace.

During the Ming Dynasties (1368-1644), not only the Forbidden City itself, but even the area between the walls of the Forbidden City and the Royal City were also closed to ordinary citizens. In the Royal City were gardens for the pleasure of the emperors and empresses, temples for them to offer sacrifices to their ancestors and pray for good harvest, offices for the ministries in charge of political, military, legal and financial affairs, and workshops and warehouses for the need of the royal family. The common men could only live in the Inner City and Outer City areas and it was in these places the alleys and lanes existed. In the mid-Qing Dynasty, the royal court gave the consent to residents of the Manchu origin to live within the Dong'an, Di'an and Xi'an gates of the Royal City, where lanes were soon to be built.

The dynastic rule came to an end in China in 1911. The gates of the Forbidden City and Royal City which had closed to the common men for nearly five centuries now opened. To facilitate transportation, the north, east and west walls of the Royal City were gradually brought

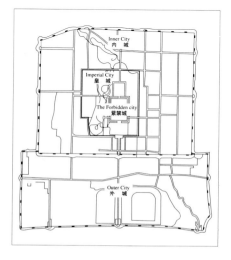

10 *Intricate Alleyways in Beijing* / 京城胡同留真

down to allow major roads to crisscross the city. Lanes between the major roads extended right to the foot of the walls of the Forbidden City in the heart of Beijing. These lanes either stretched from the Forbidden City across the moat or went closely along the city walls.

In 1995, the Municipal Government of Beijing announced plans to reconstruct the environs along both banks of the old city moat, a plan that calls for moving away the residents living between the city wall and the moat and restoring the original 17th-century layout. When that happens, the lanes in these areas will go through a fundamental change.

紫禁城下的胡同

半个世纪以前,紫禁城和胡同是北京城的两个主要组成部分。前者是旧时帝王居住的宫城;后者是平民百姓住宅的集中地,间或也有昔日王侯贵胄的府第。

紫禁城位居北京城中央,是一座城中之城。它自公元1420年建成,至1911年中国最后一个皇帝逊位,一直是皇宫禁地,今称故宫。它的四周建有高而坚固的城垣,外环深而阔的护城河,构成所谓的"金城汤池",用以防卫。除此之外,还在它的外围自内至外环筑皇城、内城,内城南垣之外又加筑外城,层层防守。

明代(公元1368—1644年),非但紫禁城周围严禁民众靠近,就连紫禁城外,皇城之内,也不能擅入。那时的皇城内建有供帝后游乐的御苑、祭祖的太庙、祭社神和谷神的社稷坛及宫前广场,掌管全国政治、军事、刑律、财政的府、部衙门,以及为皇室服务的作坊,库局也设于其内。民居只能建在内城和外城,也只有那里才有胡同。清代(公元1644—1911年)中期,朝廷允准满族居民在皇城的东安门、地安门、西安门内居住,这些地带才出现胡同。

1911年中国废除了帝制,禁锢近五个世纪的重重城门终于向寻常百姓敞开。为了便利交通,皇城东、西、北三面城墙陆续被拆除,打通了纵横交贯的干道。街道通达了,与之相连通的胡同也随之不断扩展、伸延,以至直趋紫禁城下。紫禁城下的胡同或隔护城河与宫城相望,或紧傍宫墙。阡陌街巷环拥着崔巍宏丽的宫城,四合院灰色的墙垣、黑色的屋顶映衬着红的宫墙、黄的殿顶,构成了最富有古都特色的景观。

1995年,北京市政府已制定规划,要在近几年内整治护城河两岸的环境,搬迁宫城与护城河之间的住户,使这里恢复十七世纪时的历史风貌。到时这一带的胡同势必要经历一次变迁。

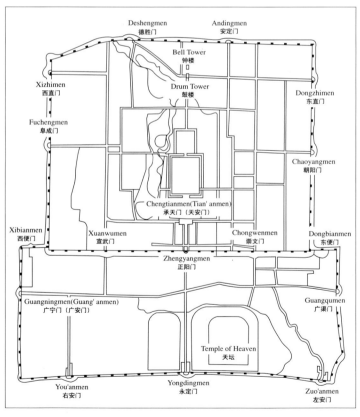

Beijing's city wall during the Ming Dynasty
明代北京城垣

Gates of the Royal Palace and Forbidden City. (*Top to botton*) Tiananmen, the middle southern gate of the Royal Palace, Duanmen, north of Tiananmen and Wumen, the south gate of the Forbidden City.

昔日皇宫门禁森严，宫门之外又设重重城门。图自上而下为皇城的正南门天安门、天安门以内的端门，以及紫禁城正南门午门。

Tourists visiting the Forbidden City. Ordinary citizens were able to enter the Forbidden City only after the abolition of the feudal dynastic system in early 20th century. It is, however, only in the last two decades that the site has experienced an influx of large numbers of tourists from China and abroad.

出入紫禁城的游人。废除帝制以后，寻常百姓才得以进入紫禁城，但是，大量中外游客来此，还是近一、二十年的事。

The Forbidden City was surrounded by a wall of 7.9 meters in height which was in return protected by a moat, giving rise to the description an "impregnable bastion".

紫禁城四周筑有高 7.9 米的城墙,墙外环凿宽而深的护城河,称之为"金城汤池"。防备森严,由此可见。

◀ A bird's eye view of the intricate structures in the Forbidden City which were arranged in one after another courtyards of quadrangle houses. The paths and passages along the palace walls resemble alleys and lanes in civilian living quarters. The real differences lie in the terrible quietness and a cold solemnity and the absence of freedom and friendship.

俯瞰紫禁城可以看出,里面的重重宫阙犹如一座座四合院,宫墙夹峙下的宫街、宫巷,形同民间的胡同,只是徒有森严与冷寂,缺少温馨与自如。

Roads extending right to the foot of the palace wall

直趋紫禁城下的道路

The rows of willow trees swaying outside the palace have long been a scenic sight in Beijing.

宫墙外,古柳成行,自古就是京城一景。

Alleys and lanes around the Forbidden City / 紫禁城下的胡同

A morning market next to the palace wall. The appearance of markets like this in recent years in Beijing makes shopping easier for the residents.

临护城河而设的早市,每天拂晓开市,近午即散。

Connoisseurs grace the antique stand at the morning market.

早市上的古董摊常有行家光顾。

The trees by the palace wall are a sanctuary for both men and birds.

人和鸟都喜欢这傍着宫墙的林荫深处。

20 *Intricate Alleyways in Beijing* / 京城胡同留真

"Check, mate!" A match at the foot of the Forbidden City.

紫禁城下布阵对弈。

"Living just an inch away from the palace."

傍城而居的人家

Alleys and lanes around the Forbidden City / 紫禁城下的胡同

Singing against the tall and solid palace wall, it is believed, produces a special acoustic effect. Thus the wall is an ideal stage for practice by Peking Opera fans.

面对高而坚实的城墙吊嗓子,能产生特殊的音响效果,因此,这里成了戏迷们的露天排练场。

The bushes and trees along the moat and the refreshing air they generate draw residents from the nearby alleys and lanes to come and do physical exercises. It is also a favorite spot for lovers.

护城河畔林木葱郁,清幽宜人。附近胡同里的居民早晚喜欢来此练拳健身,散步消闲;情侣们也视此为约会的绝佳之处。

Alleys and lanes around the Forbidden City / 紫禁城下的胡同 23

◀ The 52-meter-wide moat is so straight that people call it the "Pipe River".

护城河宽52米,堤岸笔直,京城人称"筒子河"。

The lanes next to the Forbidden City appeared after the royal palace opened to the public, thus they were, relatively speaking, younger members of the family of alleys and lanes.

紧傍紫禁城的胡同。它们应形成于紫禁城开禁以后,是胡同家族中的新生代。

Just imagine the fun of a tour along the moat on such a tricycle.

乘坐这种人力三轮车沿护城河游览,别有情趣。

26 *Intricate Alleyways in Beijing* / 京城胡同留真

A view of the royal house from a commoner's courtyard
皇家景物借入民家。

Residential houses separated from the Forbidden City by the moat.

与紫禁城隔河相望的民居

◀ A view out of the window of a residential house at Beichizi. Across the moat on the east and west sides of the Forbidden City, are Nanchizi (South Pool) and Beichizi (North Pool) and Nanchang (South Long) Street and Beichang (North Long) Street. People living in these places do not have to go out of their house to take a look at the Forbidden City.

北池子一居民家的窗外景色。紫禁城东西两侧护城河的对岸,分别是南、北池子和南、北长街,住在这里的居民足不出户就能观赏到宫城里的景物。

The physical history of the alleys and lanes

In 1370s, a new city rose in the northeast of the Middle Capital of the Kin Dynasty. Called Dadu or Grand Capital, it was the new capital for the empire known as the Yuan Dynasty. As the new city grew in prosperity, the original Middle Capital became the southern town of the new city.

In layout, the new capital city followed the traditional Confucian model of urban planning. The royal palace was situated in the southern part of the city. The city walls forming a square had eleven gates, three on each side in the east, west and south and two on the north. Inside the city, the gates led to streets twenty-five meters wide. Running from east to west and from north to south were nine streets. In each direction, joining these major streets were small streets whose width was about half of that of the major ones. On both sides of these major and smaller streets were rows of passageways, each about six to seven meters wide, then called "fire alleys" and "passageways". According to records there were 384 "fire alleys" and 29 "passageways" in the Grand Capital. Along these paths were residential houses which were divided into fifty administrative units called *fang*. Departing from past tradition of closed-off *fangs*, the new *fangs* had the streets as their boundary and cut through "fire alleys" and "passageways", laying the foundation of the street and lane arrangement of Beijing as we see today.

The southern town of the Grand Capital was built on the premises of the early town of Beijing. As early as during the Liao Dynasty (947-1125) and Kin (115-1234), the ancient capital already practiced a system of dividing the residential quarters into *fangs*. By the time the Grand Capital was built, there were already sixty-two *fangs*. Now in the southern town of the Grand Capital, streets and lanes formed a network of passageways. In fact, some of the streets and lanes could be traced back to the Tang Dynasty (618-907) and later the Liao and Kin periods.

The number of alleys and lanes grew quickly after the

Yuan emperors established and consolidated their rule. A rough counting done in 1980s pointed to more than 6,100 in the city proper and immediate suburbs.

With their different geographical locations, natural environments, time of construction and occupants, as well as imprints of history and footprints of famous residents, these alleys and lanes show a myriad spectra of natural and cultural sights and sounds, including colorful vistas of the people inhabiting these places.

胡同景观

公元十三世纪七十年代,在原金代中都城的东北郊,一座新建的城市拔地而起,它便是中国历史上元朝帝国的新都——大都城。新城落成之后,原中都城遂成为大都的南城。

新都是按照中国传统的儒家都城规制规划设计的。皇宫据于都城正南面;城垣的四方共辟十一座门,东、西、南三方各三门,北方二门。城门内建有宽约25米的干道,东西向和南北向各有九条;与大街相连的尚有小街,宽度只及大街的一半。大、小街的两侧排列着一条条宽约6~7米的"火巷"与"衚通"。据记载,大都新城内有"三百八十四火巷,二十九衚通"。"火巷"与"衚通"两旁为民宅。大都的居民区被划为50坊,这些坊打破了前朝封闭式的坊制,以街为界并经由"火巷"、"衚通"与街道相通,奠定了今日北京的胡同格局。"火巷"与"衚通"便是胡同的前身。

大都的南城位于北京最早的城址上,在它还是辽(公元947—1125年)、金(1115—1234年)都城时,城内民居就按区划分街坊,至大都新城营建前后,已达62坊。成为元大都南城之后,原来的街坊也形成了相互连通的街巷胡同。因此,这一地区有些胡同的历史可以追溯至千年以前的唐代,或稍后的辽、金时期。

元代以后,胡同逐代增加,据本世纪八十年代粗略统计,近郊区及市区的胡同街巷达6100多条,其中直接称为胡同的约1300多条。

各条胡同由于其地理位置、自然环境、形成时代、居民状况各不相同,加上在漫长的岁月中留下的许多历史印记和名人遗踪,使得这数千条胡同呈现出迥然相异的自然景观和人文景观,其中的民情世象更是千种万样。

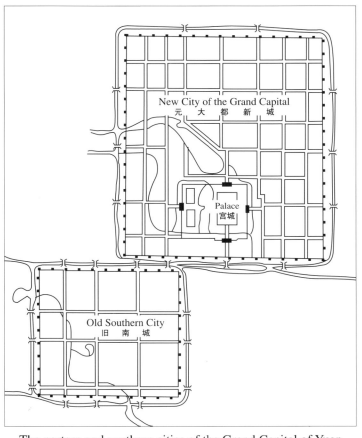

The nortern and southern cities of the Grand Capital of Yuan
元大都的南城与北城

The physical history of the alleys and lanes / 胡同景观

The lane east of the Lamaist White Pagoda in Miaoying Temple which is also known as the White Pagoda Temple. The lane on which the temple sits is called White Pagoda Lane.

白塔寺东夹道。妙应寺内有一座喇嘛式白塔,所以寺又名白塔寺,它所在的胡同则名白塔巷。白塔寺东夹道位于白塔巷以东。

Shifang Road is one of the old lanes in the West District. Over a dozen east-west lanes in the area stretch across it.

什坊小街也是西城内一条古老的胡同,呈东西走向,十余条纵向胡同与之垂直相交,布局严整。

◀ Lanes and houses near Miaoying Temple east of Fuchengmen in the West District. The temple, with a towering white pagoda built in 1279, stands in sharp contrast with the surrounding houses.

西城阜成门内妙应寺下的胡同。妙应寺建成公元1279年,其周围的胡同格局与之同时形成。

On both sides of this lane are quadrangle houses with entrances opening to the lane. Windows on the back wall of the house tend to be small, indicating the inward-looking and closed-off architectural style of these houses.

胡同两旁是古城传统的民居——四合院。院门临胡同；窗户开在墙壁上方，而且较小，呈现出内向、封闭的特点。

To admit light and facilitate communication at the time, city planners of the Yuan Dynasty set the width of the lanes in Beijing to be something equalling 9.24 meters. Even in winter, the lanes were filled up with sunlight so long as the weather was fine.

为了宜于通行和采光,元代规划的城区胡同宽度约为 9.24 米,由于两旁房舍低矮,即使在冬季,只要是晴和的日子,胡同里便充满阳光。

A small alley leading to Qianche Lane, These interconnecting alleys and lanes of different widths and lengths eventually join with the main streets, constituting a thorough transportation network in Beijing.

与前车胡同相通的小胡同。互相连通的大大小小的胡同与主要干道相接,构成了京城四通八达的交通网络。

Erlong Road in the West District was built by filling up a water way called the Erlong Pit.

在水道上填筑而成的胡同二龙路。旧名二龙坑,曾是与纵贯西城的河道相通的一条水道。

The physical history of the alleys and lanes / 胡同景观

36 *Intricate Alleyways in Beijing* / 京城胡同留真

◀ The gate tower at Qianmen, long regarded as the symbol of old Beijing. With its official name as Zhengyangmen, the gate to the center-south of Tiananmen was once the main entrance into Beijing proper. Since the 15th century, the street outside the gate has been a major commercial center in the capital.

被视为旧京象征的前门城楼。前门正名为正阳门,是北京内城的正门,位于天安门正南面。前门外大街早在十五世纪时就成为京城重要的商业区。

Called Zhubaoshi or Jewelry Market, this lane was evolved from a trading ground specializing in jewelry. There are nearly one hundred lanes radiating from the east and west sides of the Outer Qianmen Street, serving as one of the most compact and busiest commercial centers in Beijing. Many of the lanes grew from markets and fairs. Apart from the Jewelry Market, there are such lanes as Liangshidian (Grain Store), Meishi (Coal Market), Zhushikou (Jewelry Market Entrance), Roushi Street (Meat Market Street) and Xianyukou (Fresh Fish Market Entrance).

由古代的珠宝市场衍变成的胡同——珠宝市。前门外大街东、西两侧排列着数以百计的胡同,是京城内胡同最密集的地区之一。这里的胡同有许多是由当年的集市演变而成的,除珠宝市外,尚有粮食店、煤市街、珠市口、肉市街、鲜鱼口等。

The east entrance of Dashilan, one of the oldest business lanes in Beijing.

古老的商业街大栅栏东口

Stretching 370 meters, Dashilan Lane is home to a great number of traditionally famous stores including the Tongrentang Chinese Pharmaceutical Store, Ruifuxiang Cloth Shop, Neiliansheng Shoe Store and Zhangyiyuan Tea Shop.

大栅栏全长370米,两旁尽商铺,而且多是蜚声中外的老字号,如同仁堂中药店、瑞蚨祥绸布店、内联升鞋店、张一元茶叶店等。

The physical history of the alleys and lanes / 胡同景观

Dali Lane, not far from Dashilan Lane, an old commercial center, used to be called Great Li's Hat Lane. Today not only the name of the lane has changed, the hat market has disappeared too.

与大栅栏相去不远的大力胡同旧名大李纱帽胡同，原是帽市，如今名实全非。

This old shop in Grain Store Street sells a local flavor soup, *dou zhi*. Made from green beans, the soup has a special strong taste that many veteran Beijing residents love.

粮食店街内的豆汁老铺。豆汁是用绿豆制成的浆汁,味道特异,嗜食者多为京城老居民。

Liangshidian (Grain Store) Street which cuts across Dashilan Lane. In the restaurants and shops on this lane, you can find just about every kind of traditional Beijing local delicacies.

与大栅栏相通的粮食店街。街内餐馆、食肆相接,北京的风味小吃应有尽有。

The physical history of the alleys and lanes / 胡同景观

42 *Intricate Alleyways in Beijing* / 京城胡同留真

Outside the Qianmen Gate, Qingfeng Lane, a small and quiet alleyway with very little traffic. Consequently, kids can play in the lane, do graffiti on the wall and the elderly can enjoy their peace as well.

青风巷摄趣。青风巷是前门外一条僻静的小胡同,过往行人、车辆稀少,因此,儿童得以在巷中嬉戏,在壁上涂鸦;老人能够安坐无扰。

The physical history of the alleys and lanes / 胡同景观

A small lane on the diagonal Yingtao Street which is joined by many narrow alleys on both sides.

樱桃斜街中的小胡同。樱桃斜街是与大栅栏相通的一条斜胡同，两旁多窄小幽巷。

This diagonal road at the once hustling and bustling Tianqiao Market is now a very quiet alley. A group of lanes in the former southern part of the Outer City and west of the Tiantan Park are referred to as the Tianqiao Market. At the beginning of the century, some business people built seven lanes for opening up shops. By 1930s, the number of shops had grown to 773. Over a dozen theaters had also sprung up. Together they turned the place into a center of trade, catering and recreation.

曾是喧闹街市的天桥市场斜街今已成为静僻的胡同。外城南部、天坛以西，有一片名为"天桥市场"的胡同，这里便是天桥市场的旧址。天桥市场兴建于本世纪初，当时一些商民在此建起七条胡同设店经商，至30年代店铺摊贩增加到773户，并建起十几座戏园子，成为集商贸、餐饮、娱乐于一处的综合性市场。

Niujie Street and an offshoot lane. Inside Guang'anmen Gate in southwestern part of the city is a north-south street called Niujie where Moslems in Beijing live in a compact community.

牛街及通向街内的胡同之一。城区西南部的广安门内,有一条纵向的街道,名为牛街,是京城内的回族聚居区。牛街西侧由北至南排列着众多小胡同,也多以"牛街×条"命名。

The mosque at Niujie Street is a symbol of the community. Built in 995, it is the largest and oldest of its kind in Beijing.

牛街礼拜寺临街而立,成为牛街具有象征性的景观。寺建于公元995年,其规模与历史,皆为京城清真寺之冠。

A street of Moslem food shops. It is known for its large concentration of beef and mutton shops offering the freshest meat at reasonable prices.

牛街清真食品一条街。街内出售各种回族特色食品,尤以牛、羊肉的店铺、摊档最多,这里售卖的牛、羊肉肉质鲜嫩,价格低廉,闻名京城。

Elderly people dressed in Chinese Moslem attire is a common sight on this street.

漫步牛街,不时可见穿民族服装的回族老人走过。

The physical history of the alleys and lanes / 胡同景观

The 750-meter-long cultural street called Liulichang (Glazed Tile Factory) was built actually on the site of kilns producing glazed tiles for the imperial palace. The well-known stores selling traditional paintings, calligraphy works, stationery, ancient books and antiques almost are all found on this street.

古文化街琉璃厂是在为皇家烧制琉璃瓦件的窑址上兴建的,长750米。京城内经售字画、珍宝、文具、书籍等的名店几乎全集中于此。

Kongshantang and Baocuitang, two old shops dealing in antiques and jade ware.

琉璃厂内专营古玩、玉器的两家老铺——孔膳堂和宝翠堂

Interior of the theater that has been restored. Once again, people now can watch opera performances here.

修复后的戏楼内景。戏楼重现往日风貌,人们又可在此品茗观戏。

50 *Intricate Alleyways in Beijing* / 京城胡同留真

About Zhengyi Temple Theater

Built in 1667 and standing on the Xiheyan Street at Qianmen, it is the oldest theater in Beijing.

During the Ming and Qing dynasties, when people from the provinces came to Beijing either on business or to take the imperial exams, they found shelter in the Outer City outside the Qianmen and Xuanwumen gates. The provinces and counties thus built guild halls or guest houses for their folks and the Zhengyi Temple Theater was part of the Yinhao Guild Hall built by bankers and financiers from Ningbo in Zhejiang Province. Business negotiations, gatherings of friends, New Year and festival parties and sacrificial functions were often held at the place. The hall housed the God of Wealth, Zhao Gongming, with the title of Zhengyi, hence the name of the theater.

正乙祠戏楼简介

明清两代，来京城经商、科考的外省人多聚居在外城的前门外和宣武门外。各府县陆续在这一带修建供本乡旅京人员居住、联谊的会馆。较大的会馆除内设客房、厅堂以外，尚建有戏楼。正乙祠戏楼即建于前门外的银号会馆内。银号会馆为旅京浙江宁波金融界人士所建，用于立商约、联乡谊，以及年节时举行祭祀、娱乐活动，因馆内供祀正乙玄坛老祖（即财神赵公明），所以名正乙祠。正乙祠戏楼始建于公元1667年，是北京现存最古老的戏楼。

An act of a traditional Peking Opera

舞台上，正在演出京剧传统折子戏。

Opera murals inside the theater

戏楼内的戏出壁画

This mural in the theater portrays the stage and the audience during the Qing Dynasty. After a regional opera was introduced to the capital and came to be known as Peking Opera, many founders and master actors of this art performed here including such milestone figures as Cheng Changgeng, Tan Xinpei, Wang Yaoqing, Yang Xiaolou, Yu Shuyan and Mei Lanfang.

戏楼内描绘清代演出情景的壁画。自十九世纪京剧传入京城以后,许多京剧的创始人和艺术大师如程长庚、谭鑫培、王瑶卿、杨小楼、余叔岩、梅兰芳等都曾在这里登台献艺。

Yinding (Silver Ingot) Bridge crossing the merging point of Front Shishahai Lake and Houhai Lake. During the 13th century, the area near the bridge was already a major commercial district in the Yuan capital. Lanes extended from the bridge and every house faced the lake, presenting a unique sight.

横跨于什刹前海与后海交汇处的银锭桥。银锭桥一带在十三世纪时就已是元大都城内的主要商业区。桥两旁的胡同沿湖岸延展，家家宅门临水，景色宛若江南。

The diagonal Yandai (Smoking Pipe) Street, east of the Silver Ingot Bridge, twists and turns several times. Diagonal lanes like this usually were found along rivers, lakes, ditches and canals.

银锭桥以东的烟袋斜街。这是一条一街三折的斜向胡同。城区内这类斜胡同屈指可数,当初大都是沿着河、湖、沟、渠的堤岸辟建的。

Zhonglouwan (Bell Tower Twist) Lane next to the Bell Tower which stands at the north end of what used to be the central line of the ancient capital. The tower was first erected in 1272 and rebuilt in 1420. This 47.9-meter-high structure houses a big bronze bell of 5.4 meters in height. In the past, the bell was sounded twice daily, in the morning and evening, to tell the time for city dwellers.

钟楼下的钟楼湾胡同。钟楼矗立于京城中轴线的北端,始建于公元1272年,公元1420年重建。楼高47.9米,内置高5.4米的铜钟。古时每日早晚撞钟报时,城中军民、文武官员闻晨钟而起,闻晚钟而息。

A bird's eye view of Lingdang Lane from the top of the Bell Tower 从钟楼上俯视铃铛胡同。

A lane linking the bell and drum towers which are about a hundred meters apart with the Bell Tower in the north of the Drum Tower. In three stories totalling 46.7 meters, the Drum Tower was built in 1400. The second story used to house one large drum and twenty-four smaller ones, all for the purpose of telling the time.

连接钟鼓楼的胡同。鼓楼位于钟楼以南,两楼相距约百米。鼓楼建于公元1400年,高46.7米,共三层。第二层上原有大鼓一面,小鼓24面,均为古时报时而设。

The physical history of the alleys and lanes / 胡同景观

A typical scene in lanes at the foot of the bell and drum towers. Though residents of today no longer follow the bell and drum sound in arranging their activities, they lead an orderly life.

钟鼓楼下胡同里的景象

58 *Intricate Alleyways in Beijing* / *京城胡同留真*

Beihai Lane was once just a wall away from the royal park garden.

北海夹道与曾是皇家御苑的北海公园仅一墙之隔。

Beichang Street running west of the Forbidden City

地处皇城之内的北长街,纵列于紫禁城西侧。

In the morning, the food stands in a lane called West Xinglong Street are packed with customers. A tricycle rider is looking for his customers.

西兴隆街的早晨。胡同旁的早点摊座无虚席,蹬三轮的工人开始出门揽客。

Naoshikou Street running between the Inner Fuxingmen Street in the north and West Xuanwumen Street in the south used to be a thoroughfare linking the west and south districts of the capital.

闹市口街北贯复兴门内大街,南通宣武门西大街,曾是京城内连接西城与南城的重要通道。

The ancient Zhuanta (Brick Pagoda) Lane received its name from a dagoba housing the remains of the venerable Wansong Xingxiu (1165-1246), a prominent monk of Buddhism in the Yuan Dynasty at its east entrance.

古老的胡同之一砖塔胡同。位于城区西部,胡同东口立有元代佛教大师万松行秀禅师(公元1165—1246年)的墓塔,因塔为砖砌,胡同遂得此名。

Laku (Wax Warehouse) Lane still protected by animal guardians. Carved into shapes of animal heads and placed at house gates or lane entrances, the stone sculptures used to symbolize guards in keeping with an ancient tradition. Nowadays they are very rare in Beijing.

有石敢当镇守的腊库胡同。石敢当是中国民间的驱邪镇宅之物,用石料雕成兽头形状,安置在宅门上或街巷入口处,如今,在北京已成为稀有之物。

The Upper Second Lane at Huashi (Flower Market). From the 18th century, residents in the northeast corner of the Outer City made a living by selling fresh flowers or producing paper and silk flowers. At its prime time, nearly twenty lanes in this area had names related to the Flower Market. Later the market declined, but the place has maintained the name to this day.

春暖花开时的花市上二条。从十八世纪始,外城东北角一带的住户多以售卖鲜花或制作各种质料的假花为业,曾一度闻名京城,出现了近20条以"花市"为名的胡同。后来花业萧衰,市遂不存,"花市"之名却保留至今。

Primer Minister Wen's Lane outside Di'anmen Gate. Wen Tianxiang (1236-83) used to serve as prime minister of the Song Dynasty. Before the collapse of Song, Wen commanded its army to fight the Yuan troops in Guangdong. The Song army was defeated and Wen was brought to the capital, imprisoned at the Ordnance Department in this lane. Refusing to surrender, he was killed. In 1376, the Ming Dynasty which replaced Yuan had a temple built in the memory of Wen Tianxiang and renamed the lane after him.

位于地安门外的文丞相胡同。文丞相即南宋丞相文天祥（公元1236—1283年）。宋亡前夕，文天祥在广东领军与元军交战，1278年兵败被俘，后押解至大都，囚禁在这条胡同中的兵马司系械宅内，因文天祥坚不降元而被杀害。公元1376年，明朝政府在囚禁文天祥处建文丞相祠，这条胡同也随之改为现在的名字。

The Upper Fourth Lane of the Flower Market

花市上四条

Daju Lane south of the Dongzhimen Street in the northeastern part of the Inner City. The thick foliage of locust trees in the lane form an overhead green corridor.

位于东直门大街以南的大菊胡同。胡同两侧槐树成行，枝柯相交，每至夏秋犹如一条绿色长廊。

64 *Intricate Alleyways in Beijing* / 京城胡同留真

Duke Suian's Lane, named after the title bestowed by the Ming royal court to the meritorious general Chen Zhi whose residence was on this lane. There are many other lanes in Beijing that had received their names from titles of nobility.

遂安伯胡同。遂安伯是明朝勋臣陈志的封爵,因他的府第座落于胡同内,胡同遂以其爵号命名。京城多权贵,像这类以爵号命名的胡同,尚有不少。

This lane was called Hebochang, meaning a site of river and pond. The low-lying southeastern part of Beijing used to be dominated by rivers and lakes. As a result, most of the alleys, lanes and streets in this area had the words of river, lake, pond or ditch in their names. In fact, the word of Hebochang was found in the names of six lanes.

河泊厂胡同。城区东南部地势低洼,古时水泊密布,所以,这一带胡同以河、潭、淀、沟命名的居多,仅以"河泊厂"命名的就达六条。

Now called the Street of Ministry of Foreign Affairs, it used to be called Master Shi's Lane due to the fact that Shi Heng, a senior official of the Ming Dynasty, once had his house here. The residence of Mr. Shi, built in 1456, occupied a quarter of the northern side of the entire lane. In the late years of the Qing Dynasty, it was transferred into a guest house after it had changed hands several times. When Dr. Sun Yat-sen, then president of the new Republic of China, came to Beijing in August 1912, he stayed in this place. In 1913, the Ministry of Foreign Affairs moved in, giving the street the name that has lasted till today.

位居东城繁华地段的外交部街。原名石大人胡同,因胡同内有明代权臣石亨的赐第而得名。石亨府第建于公元1456年,占据胡同北侧四分之一地段。清末,这座几易其主的豪宅被改建为迎宾馆。1912年8月,中华民国第一任总统孙中山来京时曾下榻于此。1913年外交部迁入,胡同易名外交部街。

Zhengyi Road in winter and summer. About one kilometer east of the Tiananmen Square, the road is known for its European architecture, since its neighboring community was once the foreign legions.

正义路冬夏即景。正义路在天安门广场以东约1公里处,由于与旧时的使馆区毗邻,两旁建筑与街景具有欧陆风格。

Xiaojingchang Lane, next to Shijia or the Shi's Lane

与方家胡同一街之隔的小经厂胡同

Fangjia or the Fang's Lane. To name streets after family names used to be very common. Thus there were Shijia or the Shi's Lane, Liujia or the Liu's Lane, Yaojia or the Yao's Lane, Qiujia or the Qiu's Lane, etc.

以姓氏命名的方家胡同。这类胡同在京城难以计数,如史家胡同、刘家胡同、姚家井、裘家街等皆是。

The physical history of the alleys and lanes / 胡同景观

Guozijian or the Imperial College Street. The college and the Confucius Temple on the northern side of the lane were built in the 13th and 14th centuries. There are altogether four archways in the east and west entrances of the lane as well as in between. The ancient houses and archways, as well as traditional lifestyles of the residents and sturdy aged trees render the lane rich characteristics of history.

国子监街。位于安定门内,胡同北侧有十三、四世纪兴建的国子监和孔庙,胡同的东西端和胡同内共耸立着四座牌坊。古建筑群、古色古香的牌坊,衬之以古朴的民居、苍劲的街树,使得这条胡同古貌盎然。

Both sides of the archway on Shenlu Street. During the Ming and Qing periods, the entrance of major streets and lanes in Beijing were all built with archways similar to this one, as a unique architectural feature of the ancient capital city. The majority of them, however, have been torn down as they were in the way of road expansion. The one on Shenlu Street is one of the very few that still stand today.

神路街牌坊内外。明清时，京城主要街巷和胡同口都建有牌坊或牌楼，成为古城独特的街景。由于有碍交通，在扩建道路时大部分被拆除，所余仅两三处，神路街牌坊即为其中之一。

The physical history of the alleys and lanes / 胡同景观

What a gentle and harmonious turning in the lane!

弯曲如弧的胡同

The Seventh Caochang (Grass Warehouse) Lane in a summer afternoon. In the east of the Outer Qianmen Street, are ten adjacent lanes named with Caochang or grass warehouse. During the Yuan Dynasty, reeds and grass for sheltering the city wall from rain were kept here. At the time, the city wall was built with rammed earth rather than bricks and had to be covered up when it rained.

夏日午后的草厂七条。前门外大街东侧,有十条以"草厂"为名的胡同,依次纵列。这里原是元代堆放覆盖城墙的苇草的地方。因为元代城墙是用土夯筑的,每至雨季,需在墙顶覆草,以防止雨水冲刷。

Jiuwan or the Nine-Turning Lane, called so for being the lane with the most turnings.

拐弯最多的胡同——九弯胡同

Xiaolaba or the Tiny Trumpet Lane is one of the narrowest passageways in Beijing.

最窄的胡同之一——小喇叭胡同

The physical history of the alleys and lanes / 胡同景观

One of the narrow alleys built long before the age of automobiles.

在狭窄的胡同内遇有机动车通行,行人须贴壁避让。

Wow! It's only just over a meter wide.

宽仅1米余的胡同。

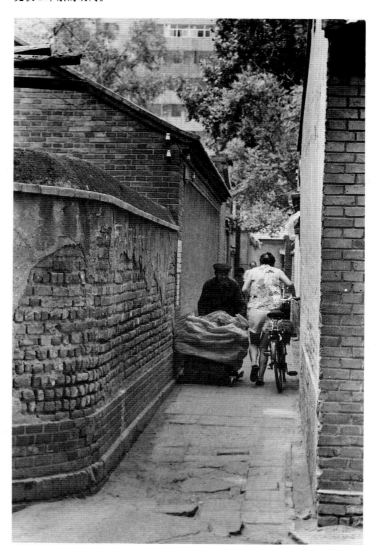

In lanes like these ones, bicycles and tricycles are the only means of transportation for the residents. After all it is not bad, for they are easy to handle and don't pollute the air.

自行车、各类脚踏三轮车是胡同里居民出行、载物的工具,这类车体积小、无污染、灵便自如,男女老少都能掌握。

A market in Zhugan (Bamboo Pole) Lane south of the Inner Chaoyangmen Street. Chaoyangmen was one of the east gates of the Inner City. At the time, all grain and other materials shipped to Beijing on the Grand Canal entered the city from this gate, to be stored either in warehouses or sold on the market. Bamboo Pole Lane was then a market for trading bamboo products which were brought over from the south.

竹杆胡同内的集贸市场。竹杆胡同在朝阳门内大街以南。朝阳门是北京内城东门之一,古时,经由大运河运往京城的粮食、货物都从此门入城,或储入仓库,或设市贸易。竹杆胡同便是当时的竹市,市上的竹子和竹器都是经运河从产竹的南方运来的。

The right means of transportation for moving about in lanes such as this.

穿行在胡同里的人力三轮车。坐这种车逛胡同最相宜。

Horse-drawn carts are about to totally disappear from the lanes forever. In ancient China, carts pulled by animals or simply bare horses and donkeys were the universal means of transportation for just about everyone from the emperor to the common man. Today, they are a rare sight.

胡同里行将绝迹的骡马车。古时候,京城内外上至帝王,下至黎民百姓,都以畜力车或驴马代步、运输;如今,这种骡马拉的大车已成了城中的稀罕之物。

The Third Dongsi Lane. Dongsi was an abbreviated name for the crossroads known as the East Four Archways which linked two major roads in ancient Beijing. During the reign of Emperor Yongle (1403-24), four archways were erected here, with one on each side, which gave rise to the name of the place. The east side of the North Dongsi Road stretching east from the crossroads was lined up with fourteen lanes, named from south to north as the First Dongsi Lane, the Second Dongsi Lane....

东四三条。东四是东四牌楼的简称,位于紫禁城北门神武门以东约1.5公里处,有纵横两条干道在此相交,明永乐年间(公元1403—1424年)在四面街口各建牌楼一座,街名由此而得。街口以北的东四北大街东侧横列有十四条胡同,由南至北依次称为东四头条、二条……

The Lesser Yabao Lane in a rainy evening. The neighborly Greater and Lesser Yabao lanes on the southern side of the Inner Chaoyangmen Street were once known as the Greater and Lesser Yaba (the mute) lanes, which were later replaced with a homonym, *yabao* (meaning elegant and precious). Such method was a common practice in changing less refined names into something more cultured and attractive.

雨夜中的小雅宝胡同。大、小雅宝胡同是朝阳门内大街南侧相邻的两条胡同,原名大、小哑叭胡同,后来利用汉语字词谐音异义的特点雅化为现名。京城胡同定名常采用这种手法化俗为雅。

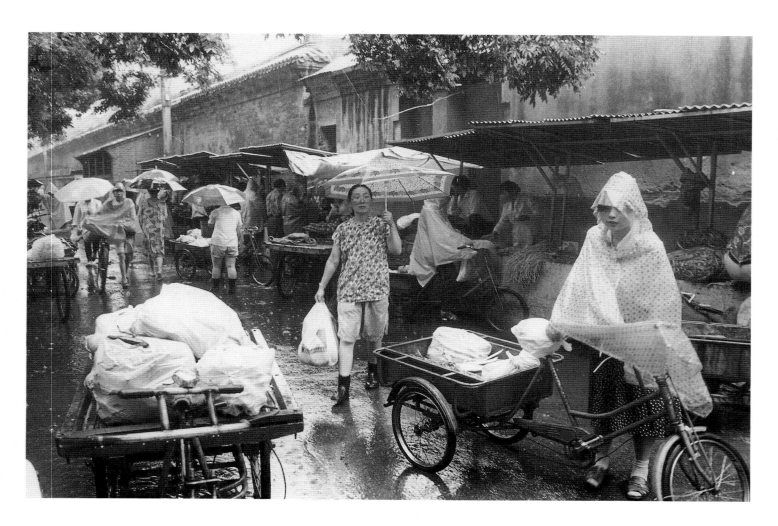

78　Intricate Alleyways in Beijing／京城胡同留真

The Greater Yabao Lane

大雅宝胡同

The physical history of the alleys and lanes / 胡同景观 79

Showers are very frequent during summer in Beijing. They come suddenly and go away in no time, giving way to fine weather again. It is convenient to take shelter from the rain in a lane--go under the eaves.

北京夏季多阵雨,往往骤然而降,须臾放晴。行人在胡同中遇雨,可就近闪入两旁的屋檐下暂避,待雨过天晴继续赶路。

Rain descends on a lane.

胡同雨景

Intricate Alleyways in Beijing / 京城胡同留真

Baofang Lane joining the South Dongsi Street in the east and Wangfujing Street in the west is said to be the site where royal families used to keep their pet leopards. No trace, however, can be found to prove this.

东接东四南大街,西通王府井大街的报房胡同,据说原是明代皇家豹房所在地。

Yanyue (concert) Lane, southeast of Baofeng Lane, was where music bands of Yuan and Ming dynasties used to play.

演乐胡同原是元明两代教坊司所属乐队演习奏乐的地方,地处报房胡同的东南。

Xiehe Lane runs between the Street of Ministry of Foreign Affairs in the south and Dongtangzi Lane in the north. Much of its original layout is still maintained to this day.

协和胡同南通外交部街,北接东堂子胡同,胡同内的格局和院落依然保持传统风貌。

82 *Intricate Alleyways in Beijing* / 京城胡同留真

The South Songnian Lane in the northeast part of the Inner City. It was once known as the Emperor's Son-in-Law Wang's Lane. In the vicinity are the East and West Songnian lanes.

内城东北的南颂年胡同,原名王驸马胡同,与其相邻的尚有东、西颂年胡同。

Thick tree foliage prevents the sun from casting its scorching rays on the Fourth Dongsi Lane.

东四四条之夏。街树枝繁叶茂,绿荫铺地,行走在胡同里暑热尽消。

Winter snow gives a face list for the Fourth Dongsi Lane.

东四四条之冬。胡同披上了银装,呈现出另一番景象。

Not a soul in sight at Shengfang Lane. This passageway whose central section turns in protrusion and then turns back again is northeast of the Street of Ministry of Foreign Affairs.

雪后的盛芳胡同寥无人踪。盛芳胡同位于外交部街东北,胡同中段呈几形。

Merely a step away from the busy and noisy Dengshikou, Baishu Lane is a sanctuary of peace and tranquility.

柏树胡同虽然与繁华的灯市口近在咫尺,却是一片宁静。

Snow brings joy to both children and adults in this lane.

冬雪给胡同里的大人和孩子带来了乐趣,打雪仗、堆雪人是儿童们最喜爱的游戏。

School is out in Xinxian Lane. There is a school every few lanes for kids in the neighborhood.

新鲜胡同里的新鲜小学放学了。每隔几条胡同便设有一所学校,学童们就近入学。

Shijia or the Shi's Lane in the East District is one of the lanes which have had the same name for more than five hundred years.

东城的史家胡同是自明代至今,五个多世纪以来,从未更易过名称的胡同之一。

Quadrangle houses in the alleys and lanes

When building the Grand Capital, the Yuan rulers stipulated that residential houses be built along the "fire alleys" and "passageways", with each family occupying no more than 0.6 hectares of land space. At the time, ordinary citizens had to pay for building their own houses, while royal families and their relatives had their houses built for them by the court. In either case, the houses took the quadrangle shape.

Quadrangle house is a most typical architectural style for residences in north China. After several centuries of existence and development, the quadrangle houses in Beijing have achieved their unique features both in layout, structure and interior decoration. Quadrangle houses are units of buildings on all four sides surrounding an inner open courtyard. The rooms in the north, reserved for elders in the family, are considered the main part. Thus they are usually larger and better decorated. The opposite ones on the east and west are for the younger members of the family. The courtyard, planted with flowers and trees, with facilities for raising gold fish and birds, is the family activity ground. In traditional Chinese societies, extended families with a strict order of seniority were favored. The compact and orderly quadrangle houses were designed for extended families in line with the concept and family life in past times.

Though all called quadrangle houses, they used to vary a great deal in size and decoration standard according to the financial resources and social positions of the owners. Ordinary residents usually lived in medium or small quadrangle houses while several or more than a dozen poor families squeezed into one courtyard. A small quadrangle house had one unit of courtyard, i.e., three bays of rooms in the north, two on each side of east and west and two to three in the south. A medium-size quadrangle house normally consisted of an inner and an outer courtyards separated by a wall and linked by a gate on the partition wall. In the inner courtyard there were more rooms and the courtyard was more spacious. In the outer courtyard, a screen faced the entrance and a series of rooms sitting on the south next to the entrance and opening to the north usually served as the study and reception room. Large quadrangle houses might include several or even more than ten units of courtyards. In some cases, gardens were built on the side or at the very back of the houses. Most of such houses in Beijing were found in the east and west of the inner city area, since during the Ming and Qing dynasties, the nobles lived in the west district and rich businessmen had their houses built in the east section of the city where commerce was more developed.

As a result of social development and population growth, it is very rare for one family to occupy a complete quadrangle house all by itself. The family order of seniority is no longer at work. The past one family-owned quadrangle houses have mostly become living quarters of a number of families with additional rooms built here and there filling up the spaces in the original courtyard. Consequently, renovation and reconstruction of the old and especially dangerous houses have become a necessity.

A bird's eye view of a medium-sized quadrangle house
中型四合院鸟瞰

1. House gate 宅门
2. Screen 影壁
3. Room opposite the main room 倒座房
4. Floral-pendant gate 垂花门
5. Circular corridor 游廊
6. Main room 正房
7. Eastern wing room 东厢房
8. Western wing room 西厢房
9. Courtyard 庭院
10. Side courtyard 跨院

胡同里的四合院

元代营建大都城时,将"火巷"与"衖通"两旁划作臣民的宅基地,规定每户只许占地八亩(约0.6公顷)。当时,百姓住房由自己出资建造,皇亲国戚的宅第由政府出资并调派工匠建造。住宅几乎全是四合院格式。

四合院是中国北方地区最具代表性的院落式住宅,而北京的四合院经过几个世纪的营建从平面布局、内部结构到细部装饰都形成了自已的特色。四合院之得名是由于其每一组建筑由东西南北四面房屋围合一个庭院组成。房屋的门窗都开向中间的庭院,以坐北朝南的北屋为正房,供长辈居住,其开间、进深、高度和装饰均为全宅之冠。东西两面相向对称布局的称东、西厢房,是晚辈的住所。庭院中栽花植树,饲养金鱼禽鸟,是全家活动的场所。中国古代社会崇尚多子多福、几世同堂,又注重长幼有序、尊卑有别,这种布局严整、主次分明的住宅正是为了适应那个时代的观念与家庭生活秩序而设计的。

同是四合院,然而其规模大小、装修规格则因宅主的财力和社会地位而异。普通民居一般为中小型四合院,贫苦的居民则几户或十几户合住一院,称"大杂院"。小四合院只有一组院落,一般有北房三间,东、西厢房各二间,南房二、三间。中型四合院多由内外院组成,两院之间有墙分隔,墙中部设门,称二门。内院房屋的间数较小四合院多,庭院也较宽敞。外院大门入口处设影壁,用以遮挡来往行人的视线。与大门相连接的一排坐南朝北的南房,俗称倒座,常用来作书房和会客之处。大型四合院由数组或十余组院落组成,有的还在住宅后部或侧面附建园林式的花园。这类四合院多集中在内城的东、西部。因为明清两代王公勋臣的赐第多建于西城,而豪商巨贾多将私宅建于商业繁盛的东城,所以旧有"东富西贵"之说。

由于社会的发展,人口的剧增,今日能独居一座四合院的人家已所剩无几,长幼尊卑各居其所的格局已不复存在,昔日布局严整的院落,多变成了墙屋相叠的大杂院。因此,对胡同及其中旧房的改造与更新势在必行。

Gate of a house on Niujie Street. A gate is built into what otherwise looks like the back of a room. The corner of the top frame and the wall often have bricks with decorations known as *ruyi*, or "as-you-wish" patterns. Thus such gates are known as *ruyi* gates.

牛街某宅大门。是另一种屋宇式的门,门设在外檐柱间,因为门楣与墙的交角处,常砌有如意形的装饰,所以称为如意门。

A spacious house entrance. Entrances of quadrangle houses consist of two main categories. One category is built into an entry way of one or several bays. The other is a gate joining two ends of the courtyard walls. The one in this photo belongs to the first category. Both sides of such an entrance have a lot of open space. Obviously, such entrances are found in expensive quadrangle houses. Usually a stone staircase outside the entrance was used for helping people to mount horses.

广亮式宅门。四合院的大门依其建筑形式分为屋宇式和墙垣式两类。前一类由一间或若干间房屋构成,后一类直接在院墙接合处设门。广亮式门属前一类,门设于屋的中柱位置,门内外皆有较宽敞的空间,用于较讲究的四合院。门前大多设有上马石。

This is another kind of entrance with two stone stools.

蛮子门是屋宇式门的又一形式,门扉位于外檐两柱之间,门框的四角为直角。

This simple kind of gate has no decorations. It is somehow called "Eagle-will-not-alight" gate.

鹰不落式院门。属墙垣式门,无多余的饰件,是较简易的宅门。

This type of entrance, joining two walls and crowned with a gate roof, is often found in small-size quadrangle houses.

墙垣式门之一。门两侧与院墙相接,门上建有门罩。较小型的四合院多采用这类形式的门。

An "Eagle-will-not-alight" gate between two low walls gives the house an air of a rural cottage.

低矮的墙垣之间嵌入一座鹰不落式的院门,使这座宅院酷似乡野的农舍。

Either patterns of plants or birds that decorate the entrance symbolize the particular interest of the dwellers.

四合院的门前或是花木扶疏,或鸟声啁啾,绿叶拂墙,屋主的情趣从中可见。

Gates of the house of the relatively well-to-do usually are decorated with door clasps, gate cymbals and protective wrappings. And in front of the entrance, there are also drum stones, stones for tying and mounting horses.

讲究的四合院门扉上饰有门簪、门钹和包叶,门前有上马石、拴马桩和抱鼓石。

98 *Intricate Alleyways in Beijing* / 京城胡同留真

Drum stones with varied decorative carvings. The lower part is a stand with a hole for resting the door axle so that the door can turn to open and shut. The drum stone, either in round or square shape, is a decorative object to expel ghost and attract good luck.

纹饰各异的抱鼓石。抱鼓石由位于门内的枕石和门外的抱鼓组成。枕石为方形,上有槽孔,门轴插入孔内,门扇就可以转动开关;抱鼓是门前的饰件,或圆或方,上面雕刻兽形或花卉图案,以驱邪纳吉。

Overhead brick carvings, which often were an indication of the social position of the house owner. A general's house would have patterns of lions playing embroidered balls, a civil official's house often had motifs of elephants and decorative objects while an intellectual's house often displayed the carvings of plants such as plums, orchids and bamboo.

门头和戗檐上的砖雕。这些雕饰往往可显示出宅主的身份,如武将一般喜雕狮子绣球,文官多雕大象或博古图案,文士则雕梅、兰、竹等图案。

Intricate Alleyways in Beijing / 京城胡同留真

Couplets carved on doors, often expressing the wish and desire of the house owner. This pair, "Honesty is the family tradition, learning is a lasting virtue" tells that this family emphasized honesty and knowledge.

镌刻在门扉上的对联。对联采用对仗、工整的联语,其内容多表达了主人的愿望和志向。

An aged tree in Shoubi Lane

寿比胡同某宅门前的参天古树

In the north-south Chaodou Lane, all the houses are arranged in a north to south direction so as to have the gates open to the south, in keeping with the orthodox architectural tradition.

炒豆胡同呈南北走向,两旁的四合院皆纵向排列,以保持坐北朝南和大门位于东南角格局。

Play-mates from the same courtyards

同院的玩伴

A traditional house now serves as a kindergarten. Some of the large and complex quadrangle houses have been turned into schools, kindergartens, clinics or other community service centers.

古宅成了幼儿园。有些规模较大的多进四合院,几经变迁成为学校、幼儿园、医疗站等社区服务机构的所在地。

Screens like this one at the entrance of a house were built to block the view of passers-by, or decorate a courtyard. Visitors just entering the courtyard could also make use of the privacy the screen provided to straighten out their outfit or make mental preparation for the meeting with the hosts.

门内的影壁。位于门的入口处,用来遮挡过往行人的视线,并可美化门庭;来访的客人入门后也可借助它的遮掩整理服饰,调整情绪。

Bamboo grown in front of a screen. On both sides of the screen flowers could be planted. Their shadows on the screen often bought out a rich decorative effect.

植于影壁前的翠竹。影壁前后可摆放盆景,栽种花木,花影映在壁上,可产生变幻丰富的装饰效果。

This seemingly iron screen dates back to the Yuan Dynasty. A stone work in the color of iron, it now stands in the Beihai Park. The Iron Screen Lane on the West Drum Tower Street was named after it.

元代遗物铁影壁。其实是一座用中性火山岩块砾石雕刻成的石影壁,色褐如铁。原立于鼓楼西大街,今移至北海公园内。鼓楼西大街至今尚有铁影壁胡同。

A screen outside the entrance. Such screens usually served the purpose of keeping the untidy part of the structure on the opposite side out of view.

大门外的影壁。这类影壁隔胡同与大门相对，用以遮挡对面房屋和屋檐、屋角等不整齐的部位。平面砌成"一"形或"冖"形。

A screen outside the entrance still stands in Sanlao Lane.

三老胡同内留存的一座大门外影壁。

A view of a screen from within the courtyard

从院内望屏立于门内的影壁。

An entrance with overhanging decorations. Under the tall roof are two overhanging "pillars" with wood carvings in between.

西城公用胡同某宅的垂花门。门上有卷棚式屋顶,两侧有一对倒悬的垂柱,两柱之间有雕花木罩。

Corridors joining an entrance with overhanging decorations

从内院望垂花门及与其相连的抄手游廊

Quadrangle houses in the alleys and lanes / 胡同里的四合院 107

This house with two courtyards on Shijia Lane was first built in the Qing Dynasty. Today, it still maintains the original layout.

史家胡同某宅内院。此宅始建于清代,为两进院落,现基本仍保持原来的格局。

Crabapple in full bloom. These trees, over a hundred years old, bear bumper harvests of fruits in the fall. They are favorite trees among Beijing residents.

庭院中盛开的海棠。海棠春天繁花满枝,秋天果实累累,树龄可逾百年,因此,京城人喜在院中种植。

Quadrangle houses in the alleys and lanes / 胡同里的四合院 109

This archway at 15 East Mianhua Lane combines architectural styles both Chinese and Western. The meticulous brick carvings feature flowers, animals and good luck patterns. Originally the residence of a Qing dynasty general named Liu, it now houses several families.

东棉花胡同 15 号宅的内宅门。为中西合璧式的拱形券门,门上砖雕精细,雕有花卉、走兽、吉祥图案。该宅原为清末一刘姓将军的住宅,现为多户居民合居。

Railing panels, baluster columns and tablet inscription on an archway.

门上的栏板、望柱和匾额

Work of fine craftsmanship

券门及侧壁上的雕刻

Quadrangle houses in the alleys and lanes / 胡同里的四合院

The main and master rooms in a quadrangle house. They are larger than other rooms in the house and stand on alleviated foundations. Always facing south, they usually consist of three to four bays and are reserved for the elder members of the family.

四合院的正房。是内宅的主房，一般有三至五间，台基和房屋都比较高大，坐北朝南，供长辈居住。

This house at 21 Xisantiao Lane near Fuchengmen was home to the great writer Lu Xun (1881-1936) from May 1924 to August 1926.

阜成门内西三条 21 号宅庭院景色。文学家鲁迅（公元 1881—1936 年）曾于 1924 年 5 月至 1926 年 8 月寓居于此。

Rearranged as what it was like when Lu Xun lived here

鲁迅旧居室内的格局与陈设仍按当年原样布置。

Quadrangle houses in the alleys and lanes / 胡同里的四合院

The house at 19 Fengfu Lane in the East District was the residence of the late author Lao She (1899-1966). A native of Beijing, he lived for sixteen years in this house, where he produced twenty-three novels and dramas, mostly based on the history of Beijing with languages typically spoken by Beijingers.

老舍故居——东城丰富胡同19号宅。现代小说家、戏剧家老舍(公元1899—1966年)生前在这座小院内居住了16年,写出《方珍珠》、《龙须沟》、《西望长安》、《茶馆》等23部作品。

A very ordinary screen shuts off the noise of the street and gives peace to the Red Persimmons Courtyard.

一座极平常的影壁将纷扰的市声挡在门外,使丹柿小院拥有一份清幽。

The main rooms of Lao She's residence. He and his wife, Hu Jieqing, planted the two persimmon trees, which gave the courtyard the name of "Red Persimmons Courtyard".

故居的正房。房前有两棵柿树,为老舍与夫人胡絜青手植。小院因树得名,称"丹柿小院"。

114 *Intricate Alleyways in Beijing* / 京城胡同留真

A corner of the courtyard

小院一角

Sitting room doubling as study. The books and stationery indicate the learning of the house owner.

简朴的客厅兼书房。里面书籍盈柜积案,显现出主人的高情远致。

Mei Lanfang, master Peking Opera actor, used to live here at 9 Huguosi Lane, now Mei Lanfang Memorial Museum.

护国寺胡同9号宅内分隔内外院的垂花门。该宅为京剧艺术大师梅兰芳先生故居,今辟为梅兰芳纪念馆。

Corridor in a house in West Rongxian Lane

西绒线胡同某宅跨院中的游廊

Quadrangle houses in the alleys and lanes / 胡同里的四合院

This gate with overhanging decorations in Prince Gong's Palace leads to a garden in the northern part of the premise. Covering 28,000 square meters, the garden has more than twenty scenic attractions.

恭王府花园内的垂花门。花园位于府邸以北，面积 2.8 万平方米，有 20 余处景点。

Introduction to Prince Gong's Palace

This house on West Qianhai Street at Shishahai is the most well protected of all the residences occupied by princes of the Qing Dynasty. Shishahai is a narrow long lake in the northwestern part of the West District. Its green trees and rippling waters and closeness to an imperial garden made it a favorite spot for building houses by the rich and noble. No wonder there are many ruins of houses formerly belonging to imperial family members.

Built in 1777, it was the private residence of He Shen, a corrupt official and protege of the Qing Emperor Qianlong (1736-96). Soon after the death of the emperor, He Shen was arrested and sentenced to death in 1799. This house was confiscated and became known as Prince Qing's Palace for a while. In 1851, it was given to Prince Gong, thus its name.

恭王府简介

恭王府是北京现存清代王、公府邸中保存最完整的一座，位于什刹海前海西街。什刹海是城区西北部一狭长形湖泊，这里翠柳环堤，碧水溶溶，又地近皇家御苑，自古以来历代的皇亲国戚都喜欢在湖畔建府造园，因此，沿海胡同内多豪宅王府的遗址。

恭王府约建于 1777 年，原是清乾隆帝的宠臣和坤的私宅。1799 年，和坤因罪被处死，府第被没收曾一度改为庆王府。1851 年改赐恭亲王奕䜣，遂称恭王府。

A moon gate in the garden

恭王府花园中的月洞门

A lake and a mid-lake pavilion in the garden of Prince Gong's Palace

园内的池塘和湖心亭

Quadrangle houses in the alleys and lanes / 胡同里的四合院

An alley in the palace which consisted of the central, east and west sections, separated by the east and west alleyways. Each section has several courtyards.

府邸中的夹道。府邸由中、东、西三组建筑群组成,每一组皆拥有多进四合院。东西两夹道位于三组建筑群之间。

Corridor in the garden
花园中的游廊

122 *Intricate Alleyways in Beijing* / 京城胡同留真

Site of a garden in a residential house on Weijia Lane. Once a large quadrangle house with a garden, it was designed by Ma Huitang, an architect in the last years of the Qing Dynasty. The garden was complete with intricately-arranged rockeries, lake, corridors, flowers and trees. Now home to a number of families, its former splendor, unfortunately, no longer exists.

魏家胡同某宅花园遗址。该宅原是一座附有花园的大型四合院,由清末著名营造家马辉堂设计。花园内假山、湖池、游廊、花木配置有致,可惜现已成多户居民合住的杂院,失去了原有的韵致。

Tile ends in quadrangle houses often feature meticulous patterns. Most of the quadrangle houses were built with the same kind of bricks, tiles and timber that had been in use for more than two thousand years. Tile ends with patterns like these were already extensively used during the Qin Dynasty (221-206 BC).

四合院檐头的瓦当。京城四合院的建筑材料是两千多年以来沿用的砖瓦和木材,这种模印花纹的瓦当在两千多年前的秦、汉时期就已广泛运用。

Only part of the wooden windows in quadrangle houses use glass. The rest part is pasted with a particular kind of thick white paper in spring, fall and winter and window screening in summer.

四合院居室的窗大都是木格窗棂,局部镶嵌玻璃,其余部分春、秋、冬三季糊白麻纸,夏季换装透气的窗纱。

Interior in an ordinary family house

平常人家的居室陈设

Traditional interior arrangement. The horizontal chest is for keeping clothes. Porcelain ware and vases in pairs, along with a mirror and clock, serve as interior decorations. Today such arrangement can only be found in very few houses of long-time Beijingers.

传统的室内陈设。木质的横柜,内放衣物;柜上对称地陈列着瓷罐、花瓶、钟、镜等。现在除了极少世居京城的老人,已无人这样布置居室了。

The coal stove serves as the heater. Winter arrives in Beijing in November and heating facilities have to be installed in the room. Stoves like this are found in most small and medium-size quadrangle houses.

拥炉取暖。每年11月北京进入冬季,气温骤降,室内需要设置取暖设施。中、小型四合院一般用煤炉取暖。

There is a public running water tab in each courtyard. Sometimes, water freezes inside the pipe in winter. The lady is pouring hot water to defrost the pipe water.

每一院内设有公用的自来水龙头,冬季管内的水常常冻结,取用前须浇热水融化。

Removing night soil from a toilet in a quadrangle house courtyard, now inhabited by a number of families. Without modern facilities, these houses still depend on this rather primitive arrangement.

大多数四合院卫生设施陈旧,尚用原始的方法清除粪便。在四合院里常能遇上身背粪桶为居民除秽清污的掏粪工人。

Population in Beijing has been on a sharp increase in the last several decades. People have to build additional rooms in originally neatly-laid out courtyard.

杂院一角。近数十年来京城人口急剧增加,原本布局疏朗的四合院内不断添房加屋,成了多家共居的大、小杂院。

For centuries, pigeon raising has been a lasting hobby of Beijing residents.

栖息在屋檐上和庭树枝头的鸽群,飞翔于蓝天的鸽影,是京城胡同内自古至今从未消逝过的景色。

A view outside the rear window

后窗外的风景

A gold fish container. Rich or poor alike, Beijingers love to raise gold fish as a spare-time hobby. In fact, people have summarized typical sights in a courtyard of quadrangle house as "canopy of plants, fish containers and pomegranate trees".

居室一角的金鱼缸。京城人都喜欢饲养金鱼以自娱,所以,有人将四合院中的景物概括为"天棚鱼缸石榴树"。

Things to help tide over the long winter. Coal for heating, cabbage which is good to eat and easy to keep, seasonings such as garlic and peppers are kept under kitchen eaves. This corner is a true reflection of the life of Beijing residents living in small lanes.

家居越冬的必备之物。取暖用的煤、易于存放而又百吃不厌的大白菜、调味用的蒜头和辣椒都陈放于厨房外的屋檐下。虽然是四合院中小小的一角,却是京城百姓生活一斑的真实写照。

Vegetables are for decorating the environment rather than consumption. They give one the impression of being in a rural dwelling placed in the middle of an urban center.

院中瓜瓞累累,令人顿生"居城如在野"之感。

Gourd grown under a house eave

屋檐下的葫芦架

132 *Intricate Alleyways in Beijing* / 京城胡同留真

No matter how difficult the living conditions are, residents in Beijing always manage to build up a green environment.

京城人不论居住条件优劣,都能因地制宜营造出一片绿色的空间。

To watch snow turning the courtyard into a work of contrasting bright and dark colors from the well-heated room is a great fun for residents in Beijing.

坐在暖融融的屋内,隔窗望着晶莹、绵密的雪花将庭院中的景物勾勒成明暗鲜明的画幅,是京城人冬日里的一桩乐事。

The first snow in the year has descended while persimmons are still in the trees. The orange-color fruit and snow create a beautiful sight.

橙红色的柿子尚挂在枝头,第一场冬雪已经降落。柿红雪白,庭院里展现出一幅绚丽的图画。

What a change from the grey-color lanes!

大雪过后,灰色的胡同变成了粉妆玉琢的无垢世界。

Life in the alleys and lanes

Alleys and lanes in Beijing have their particular charm. Once you walk into one, even if it is just steps away from the hustle and bustle of the urban center, you will find that the noise is completely shut out. Instead, you will find a unique atmosphere of peace and tranquility, a rich traditional friendly human relationship and encounter easy-going residents.

Despite the change of time, the alleys and lanes have always been the house of the ordinary. Here, they live, labor and raise their families. Here, they enjoy their pleasure and experience the hardships in life. So this way, life has been going on from generation to generation. It may seem rather ordinary and dull, but life here embodies a rich culture.

Soon after a town was built three thousand years ago in the area which today Beijing stands, the place became a favorite spot for ethnic groups in north China. In the last 700 to 800 years, it has served as the capital of China, a center of politics and culture for the country. Officials, businessmen, intellectuals, artists and artisans from all over the country or even from other nations came and lived here, bringing along with them cultural heritages and customs which were absorbed and merged with the indigenous way of life, enriching the already colorful culture. The way of life, customs and habits, festival celebrations, rituals, fashions and business codes in the alleys and lanes were all reflections of a particular culture.

Beijing has many festivals, the major ones being the Spring Festival, the Lantern Festival, the Dragon Boat Festival, the Mid-Autumn Festival, the Double Nine (9th day of the 9th month on the lunar calendar) Festival and the New Year's Eve. To residents not living in lanes, the customs and habits associated with these festivals are fading away with the onset of modern concepts, but they retain their glamour and importance in the alleys and lane.

Since ancient times, it has been a custom for residents in alleys and lanes to cultivate flowers and trees, raise gold fish and birds, as a way to improve the environment and cultivate their personalities. According to historical materials, there was a bird market during the Yuan Dynasty. In the spring of 1323 alone, the government bought 100,000 birds raised by the residents and set them free, indicating the huge number of birds people must have kept at the time. Despite changes in many ways, people have till this day maintained the tradition of bird raising.

Living in compact neighborhood, people in the alleys and lanes have developed a close and friendly relationship. Mutual help has been a way of life till today.

The alleys and lanes have always been the ground for peddlers and craftsmen, who tour the lanes, shouting their wares and services at the top of their voice or beating out particular sounds to attract customers among the residents. Gradually, the sounds they make has become a unique feature of Beijing, unforgettable to those who have had the experience of living in alleys and lanes.

胡同风情

作为一种生存景观，北京的胡同自有它令人依偎与流连之处。只要一走进胡同，那怕咫尺之外就是车水马龙的闹市，喧嚣也会顿时全消，所感、所见的是沉静、恬淡的氛围，淳厚亲切的人情味，悠然自得、乐天知命的居民。

不论哪个时代，胡同都是最基层的民众的栖身之地。他们在这里生息、劳作、繁衍，在这里享受欢娱，经历痛苦，一代又一代，周而复始。看似平淡无奇，而其中却蕴涵深厚的文化内容。

自三千多年前北京地区有城邑以来，就是中国北方各民族的聚居地。近七八百年，它成为帝都和共和国的首都，成了中国政治、文化的中心，来自全国乃至世界各地的官员、商贾、知识分子、艺术家、工匠长期旅居于此，各地的文化和习俗风尚也随之传入并为本土文化所吸纳、融合，使原本就蕴涵深厚的文化更加多彩多姿。胡同里所特有的节令习俗，民情世风、人生礼仪、时尚娱乐、商情市声等，都是这种文化的具体表现。

北京传统的节令很多，主要的有春节、元宵节、端午节、中秋节、重阳节、除夕等，与这些节日相伴随的乡风土俗丰富多彩。随着现代意识的渗入，胡同以外的居民对此已渐趋淡化，而胡同里的节日气氛依然浓郁。

胡同里的居民自古就喜欢栽花植树，饲养禽鸟、金鱼，藉以美化环境，怡情养性。据记载元大都就已设有鸟市，市民所养之鸟，不可数计。仅1323年春，政府为了放生，一次就从市民手中收买笼禽10万只。由元至今，世事沧桑，而市民的这些好尚却没有改变。

胡同里家家户户门户相望，又都出入于一条胡同，时时相遇，相处得融洽亲密。邻里之间疾病相扶，患难相救，这种风气自古至今延绵不绝。

胡同里向来就是小商贩和手艺人的出没之地，他们穿行于胡同之中，用高亢悠长的叫卖声和敲击不同响器声，招引四合院里的居民出来购买，久而久之形成了胡同里特有的市声，常令许多在胡同里住过的人终生难忘。

"Acting as the Bride". Despite all other games of modern times, girls in this lane still favor this traditional game of pleasure seeking.

扮"新娘"。尽管现代化的玩具和游戏方式层出不穷,胡同里的女童却对古老的游戏情有独钟。

Taking the first step of his life this way, just like all others who grow up in small lanes.

生长在胡同里的人,几乎都是像这样迈出人生第一步的。

Life of a future football star may well begin from a lane.

未来的"国脚"也许就来自这里。

Small lanes have their own traffic rules.

在胡同里行走或休憩,除须遵守公共交通规则以外,尚有其约定俗成的规矩,即相互礼让,各不相扰。

Here in the lanes they have endless sources of subjects for sketches.

胡同里世象纷呈,是写生的最佳处。

Only the young and old have time to relax during the day at South Jixiang Lane.

南吉祥胡同里的老人和孩子。白日里有暇在胡同里闲坐或玩耍的,只有老人和孩子。

Loving to keep pets such as dogs, cats, monkeys and rabbits, Beijing residents favor dogs and cats more than other animals. Recently, the city tightened rules in regard to dog raising to ensure public hygiene and safety.

犬趣。京城人喜欢饲养犬、猫、猴、兔等小动物,尤以养犬、猫的人家最多。近年市内实行限制养犬的规定,以保障城市卫生和市民安全。

A flower seller makes his round in a lane.

走街串巷的卖花人

142 *Intricate Alleyways in Beijing* / *京城胡同留真*

Newspaper stories suggest Beijing residents have a history of several hundred years in raising katydids. Every turn from summer to fall, farmers from the suburbs or neighboring provinces come in Beijing loaded with this kind of longhorned grasshoppers to sell to city kids. The result, katydids singing is heard from every courtyard.

夏秋之交,京郊以及外省农民挑着整担的蝈蝈沿胡同叫卖,引得孩子们争相购买,一时间,家家户户都传出秋虫的鸣叫声。据记载京城人养蝈蝈已有几百年的历史了。

Bird raising is a great hobby in Beijing and bird singing can simply be heard in just about every household. In recent years, environmental protection organizations have been appealing to the residents to let free their caged birds. Still, it will be sometime before bird lovers are ready to give up their caged pets.

京城养鸟之风炽盛,胡同里几乎家家闻啼鸟。近年一些环境保护组织呼吁市民们放鸟归林,但是,要使众多的恋鸟者割舍人鸟之情,恐尚要假以时日。

Retirees often find pleasure from bird raising. Every morning they take their birds to parks or woods so that the birds can have a moment of pleasure of being in the natural environment.

赋闲的老人多以养鸟自娱,每日清晨要到公园或林木繁茂的地方遛鸟,让笼中的鸟儿享受返归自然的短暂快乐。

Intricate Alleyways in Beijing / 京城胡同留真

Let the birds enjoy the winter sunshine.

享受冬日的阳光

This old man, more than seventy years old, from Chuantangmen Lane has been raising birds for several decades.

家住穿堂门胡同的这位七十余岁的老人,几十年与鸟相随相伴,结下了不解之缘。

Nothing can make him happier than strolling with his birds.

乐在其中

Life in the alleys and lanes / 胡同风情

More skilled kite lovers find the small lanes too narrow for the sport. For them, the Tiananmen Square is a better choice of location.

一些放风筝的高手嫌胡同狭窄不能尽兴，便来到天安门广场一显身手。

To fly kites in the spring or fall is a favorite sport for many Beijing residents. Colorful kites can be seen in the sky over small lanes.

在春风和畅和秋高气爽的日子里放风筝，是京城人的一件乐事。每逢此时，胡同的上空飘荡着各色各样的风筝。

Going with grandpa on a walk for the birds. It is in this way that the tradition is passed on.

跟爷爷去遛鸟。京城人的好尚就是在这样的熏染下,一代代延续下来的。

To keep pets is a fashion for young residents in Beijing.

饲养宠物成为年青人的时尚。

A holiday morning at the entrance of the West Taiping Street. These pictures were taken from 8:00 to 9:00 one holiday morning.

假日的西太平街路口。摄于上午8至9时。

Life in the alleys and lanes / 胡同风情

Three generations living in harmony

三代同堂,其乐融融。

A popular game of both joy and scare. To set off firecrackers, for centuries until a few years ago, had always been associated with holidays in Beijing. Now it is banned in urban districts.

又喜又惧观燃炮。在喜庆的节日里燃放鞭炮,曾是京城自古就盛行的习俗,近年市内实行禁放规定,城区从此不闻鞭炮之声。

Life in the alleys and lanes / 胡同风情

One wedding and the entire lane is filled with a festival mood.

胡同里的婚礼。一家有喜事,左邻右里都来帮忙、祝贺,整条胡同都洋溢着喜庆气氛。

With the introduction of Western way of life, white wedding gowns have replaced traditional wedding apparel, and bridesmaids have been replaced by the best men. Weddings in small lanes are becoming a combination of Chinese and Western practices.

西风东渐,白色的婚纱取代了传统的嫁衣,伴娘改为傧相,胡同里的婚礼已演化成中西合璧式的了!

A bride arrives at her new home at Beita Lane.

花市中三条的迎亲场面

Merry making in the nuptial room is a traditional practice and still maintains its popularity today.

新婚之夜闹新房是中国传统的婚俗,至今仍是婚礼中不可少的节目,也是婚礼的高潮。

To watch street activities, chat about today and talk about yesterday: a way of life for elderly men from small lanes.

看街景、谈天说地、感今抚昔,是胡同里老年男子的消闲方式。

Grandma and her grandchildren

老来孙作伴

Intricate Alleyways in Beijing / 京城胡同留真

Life in the alleys and lanes / 胡同风情   157

A veteran carpenter telling his past

老木工话说当年

Enjoying themselves

自得其乐

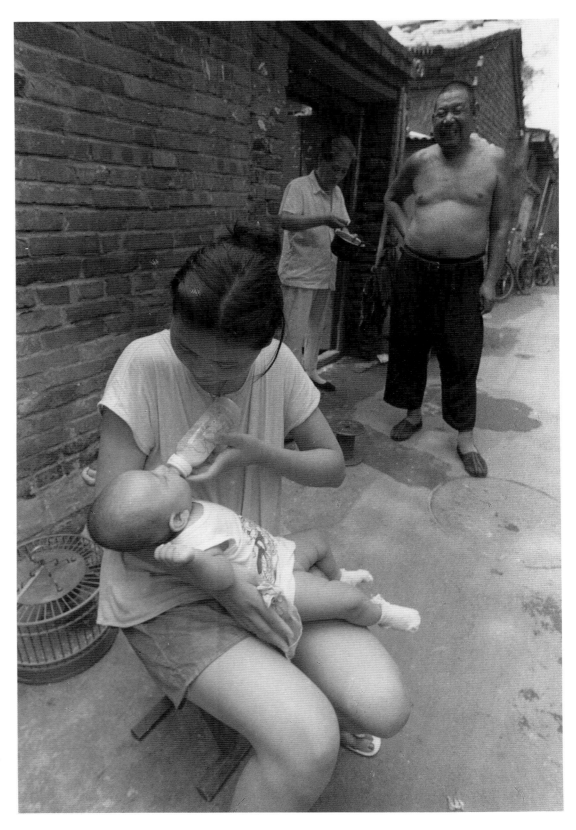

A new member in a family from a Beijing lane

家族的新成员

Residents in small lanes near Shishahai Lake are uniquely located. In winter, they go skating or winter swimming and in summer they enjoy swimming and viewing lotus plants.

160　*Intricate Alleyways in Beijing* / 京城胡同留真

住在什刹海附近胡同里的居民得天独厚,冬季可在湖上溜冰、在湖中游泳,夏季则可临湖观荷。

Sugarcoated haws are popular on the ice too.

卖冰糖葫芦的小贩直趋冰上,招徕买主。

According to tradition, on every 22nd of the last month on the lunar calendar, people in Beijing paste up Spring Festival couplets and portraits of the door gods. Both the couplets and portraits can be easily found at business stands in lanes, big or small, near Qianmen.

京城旧俗,每年农历十二月二十二日,家家户户须换贴新春联、门神,以迎新纳福。在此前后大街小巷都有售卖春联、门神的摊点。

In Beijing, water melons are a favorite fruit in summer. Farmers deliver their produce to the door in lanes on the edge of the city.

西瓜是京城市民的消暑佳品,瓜熟时节,京郊的瓜农运瓜入城,沿胡同叫卖,成为夏日一景。

A coal mill in a small lane. Coal shaped in this fashion is referred to as the honeycomb coal, which is easy to burn and keep. In the past decade, it has been a major fuel for residents in Beijing.

胡同里的煤厂加工制作蜂窝煤,供应居民。

164 *Intricate Alleyways in Beijing* / 京城胡同留真

Helping Daddy to get a filled-up gas cylinder. Some residents use gas as fuel and have to take the empty cylinder for a full one at the gas station in the neighborhood.

帮爸爸换煤气。部分居民用罐装的液化煤气作燃料,罐内煤气用完后,可到距家最近的煤气供应站购买。

Delivering coal. The honey-comb coal can be ordered at a nearby coal mill which will deliver the order to the door.

送煤到户。用户所需的蜂窝煤可到附近的煤厂订购,由煤厂派送煤工送到家中。

Life in the alleys and lanes / 胡同风情

A key cutting stand

修锁配钥匙的小摊，早设晚收。

Cotton fluffing, a job done by people from outside Beijing, who tour the city, doing business with a fluffing bow.

弹棉花。操此业的都是来京谋生的外地人,他们凭着一张竹弓,走遍京城招揽生意。

Advertising for service. The tools used and the way people who sharpen kitchen choppers and scissors advertise are exactly the same as described in folk paintings over a hundred years ago.

敲着响器走街串巷的磨刀剪匠人。其所用的工具与招揽主顾的方式与一百多年前民俗图中所绘毫无二致。

Colorful dough figures are no less attractive than electronic toys.

用各色面团捏成的面人对儿童们的吸引力不逊于电动玩具。

Fascinated by a craftsman blowing a syrup figure.

看吹糖人的艺人现场制作,令这个小女孩着了迷。

168 *Intricate Alleyways in Beijing* / 京城胡同留真

Looking better than they taste

手工制作的糖花味道平平,造型却十分夸张。

Making sweet glutinous rice flour dumplings in a lane for the Lantern Festival. The round shape of this delicacy eaten on the 15th day of the 1st month on the lunar calendar symbolizes reunion of the family and smooth sailing in people's life and career. To prepare them, the fillings are made into small balls and shaken in wet glutinous rice flour until the fillings are securely wrapped up. Then they are ready to be boiled and served.

胡同里现摇现卖的元宵摊。中国农历正月十五日是民间的元宵节,这一日晚上家家都要吃元宵,以求一年之中家人团聚,事事圆满。北京制作元宵的方法颇为独特,先将调好的馅搓成团,而后放在浸湿的糯米粉里摇滚,让糯米粉逐层裹于馅外。

Life in the alleys and lanes / 胡同风情

Fruits from both the north and south of the country are available in stands at entrances of small lanes.

胡同口的水果摊上南北鲜果,四季不断。

Shishkabab was introduced to Beijing from the northwest region of Xinjiang twenty years ago.

街头小吃烤羊肉串是近一、二十年才由新疆传入京城的。

A special kind of porridge called literally "flour tea" instantly made and served. To make this traditional Beijing delicacy, wheat flour is first baked and then added with ground peanut, walnut, sesame and sugar. To serve, pour in boiling water and make the flour mix into a thick broth. The copper pot containing boiling water is heated with coal from the center tube. Its mouth is cast into the shape of a dragon head, giving it the name "dragon-head copper pot".

即食即冲的面茶,香气扑鼻。面茶,又名茶汤,是京城传统的风味食品。制法是先将面粉炒熟,搀入捣碎炒熟的花生、核桃仁、芝麻和白糖,吃时将炒面放入碗内,冲入沸水调合成糊状。烧水用特制的大铜壶,壶中有膛,用来燃煤烧水;壶嘴铸成龙头形,俗称"龙嘴大铜壶"。

Humorous and interesting donkey performance is very popular at temple fairs during the Spring Festival in Beijing.

诙谐、风趣、富有乡土气息的跑驴表演是京城春节庙会上必有的节目。

Lion dance at the temple fair held at Beijing's White Cloud Temple, the largest holy ground of Taoism in the city. Located near Fuxingmen in the West District, it has been known for its temple fairs for centuries.

白云观庙会上的舞狮表演。白云观是京城最大的道观,位于西城复兴门外,这里的春节庙会自古就享誉京城。

These performers walking on stilts, doing donkey dance and lion dance are farmers from suburban Beijing. On festival occasions, they often come in the city, bringing their skill and laugh.

踩高跷。踩高跷、跑驴、舞狮的表演者大都是京郊农民业余演出队的成员,他们农闲时排练,遇有节庆前来助兴。

174 *Intricate Alleyways in Beijing* / *京城胡同留真*

"Visiting the Temple Fair on Donkey Back" is a performance at the White Cloud Temple Fair to show how people celebrated in the past. Until 1920s and 1930s, donkeys were a popular means of transportation when Beijingers went out of the city. The White Cloud Temple was on the edge of the city at the time. Naturally many easily came to the fair on donkey backs.

白云观庙会上的娱乐项目"骑驴逛庙会"。直至本世纪二、三十年代,京城人到郊外出游,仍以毛驴或马车代步。白云观地处城郊,当年逛庙会都骑驴而至。为重现旧时风情,近年庙会上增设了这项游娱。

Whole families making dumplings together on the New Year's Eve and eating them at mid-night is an age-long tradition.

京城古俗,除夕之夜家人围坐一处包饺子,待到夜半子时煮食,称为"交子"。这一习俗一直沿袭至今。

Sun Baocai (*left*), known as one of the "new magic actors" of Tianqiao area in a comic performance. Lanes near the original Tianqiao Market were where artists of all arts used to perform. Many extremely talented people started their career here. Together they were referred to as "magic performers of Tianqiao".

天桥的新"八大怪"之一孙宝才(左)在表演双簧。天桥一带的胡同是原天桥市场所在地,这里曾是诸般艺人荟萃之处,各个时期都出现过一些身怀绝技、行貌奇特的艺人,人们统称为"天桥八大怪"。

Life in the alleys and lanes / 胡同风情

For this man of superb breathing exercise skills, his head remains unhurt after the bricks hitting his head are smashed into pieces.

气功表演劈砖。头顶的砖被劈得四分五裂,顶砖的人却毫发无损。

178 *Intricate Alleyways in Beijing* / 京城胡同留真

The accuracy with catapult has also been a traditional skill displayed at Tianqiao.

弹弓功绝技也是当年天桥市场上表演的传统武艺之一。

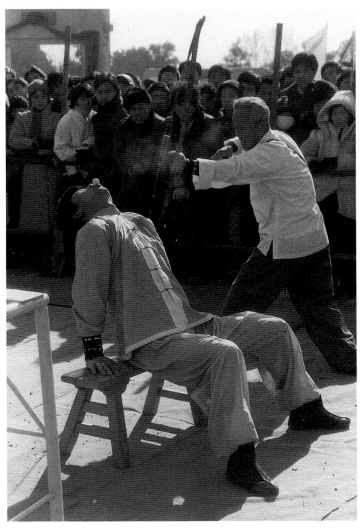

Well-versed actors of deep breathing exercises can endure the attack of sharp weapons unscathed.

天桥传统绝技之一——气功表演刀枪不入。

Life in the alleys and lanes / 胡同风情

Changes in the alleys and lane

Since the end of 1980s, the Municipal Government of Beijing has embarked on a program of renovating and repairing old and dangerous living quarters in the alleys and lanes. A major measure of modernization in this ancient city, the endeavor means an effort of change which is unprecedented both in scope and speed since the lanes ever came into being in the 13th century. Often in a matter of days, houses on one or several lanes are levelled to the ground and two to three years later, tall buildings or spacious roads appear instead. Thus, many old alleys and lanes disappear or change face. While sighing helplessly for the disappearance of these historic landmarks, people can only console themselves with this reasoning: To replace the old with the new is always a price any city has to pay in the process of modernization.

In old house renovation, some residents have to live temporarily elsewhere before new houses are completed on their home ground. Others directly move into new housing areas in the suburbs. To move out of dilapidated and crowded one-story houses into new apartments complete with utilities should be a dream coming true. Yet, once their dream does come true, they find it hard to completely leave the old dwellings. Beyond the joy of moving into new apartments from old brick rooms, they feel an indescribable sense of loss as they can no longer step out of the room into the self-entertainment of cultivating flowers in the courtyard garden or meet and talk every day with neighbors who are as dear as family members.... In short, they have better and more comfortable living spaces, but they have lost the kind of intimate environment and ease of life found in the lanes.

In response to this state of mind of the residents, urban construction departments, designers and architects have begun the search for new design plans to allow the renovated and new residential quarters to suit the way of life of Beijingers and maintain the traditional customs in the alleys. Apartment buildings that try to maintain the traditions of residential houses in Beijing in layout, structure, color and interior design have appeared in recent years. The housing projects at Xiaohoucang Lane in the West District and those resembling the style of quadrangle houses in Juer Lane in the East District are some of these examples.

胡同的变迁

自本世纪八十年代起,北京市政府开始实施对胡同及其中的危旧房改造的规划,这是古城现代化进程的重大举措。九十年代,这种改造在各城区全面展开,其覆盖面之广、进度之快,是自十三世纪胡同格局形成以来未曾有过的。往往数日之间一条或一片胡同即被夷为平地;一年或两、三年后,现代化的楼群便代之而起。诸多古老的胡同就此消失、改观。人们在喟叹失去历史陈迹的同时只能这样自慰:除旧布新,这是每一个走向现代化的都市都须付出的代价。

危旧房改造过程中,里面的一部分居民暂时借居他处,等待在原地重建新居;有的则迁至近郊区新落成的居民小区内。离开残旧、拥挤的平房,迁入设施完善的楼房,本是胡同里众多居民企盼已久的事,然而,一旦梦想成真反而难以割舍对老屋和胡同的依恋。待到从古旧的砖瓦房迁入凌空而立的住宅楼之后,在欣喜之余又都不免感到一种难以言喻的失落:失去了举步就能走到院中侍花弄草的乐趣,又不能日日与亲如家人的邻居声息相闻……总之,有了舒适与宽敞,却失去了亲切与自如。

了解到市民的这种心态之后,市政部门和建筑师们即开始探求一种新的设计方案,以求改建后的住宅既能适应北京人的居住习惯和心理特点,又能保持胡同原有的古老风貌。近几年已建造出一批在结构、布局,以至外墙色调和细部装饰都富有北京民居特色的住宅楼,如西城小后仓的楼群、东城菊儿胡同的四合院式住宅楼,都属此类。

Another group of lanes have been flattened.

又一片胡同被夷为平地。

These old quadrangle houses have to go, too.

正在拆除的四合院群。

Changes in the alleys and lanes / 胡同的变迁

Disappearing quadrangle houses

一座即将消失的四合院。

The old is replaced by the new.

除旧布新

Remaining traces of warm and peaceful family life

残壁上还留有家的温馨。

Hard to leave!

故宅难舍

186 *Intricate Alleyways in Beijing* / 京城胡同留真

New houses at Juer Lane have maintained some of the architectural features of traditional quadrangle houses.

菊儿胡同内新建的住宅楼采用了四合院的建筑格局。

Afterword

by Shen Yantai

I am from south China, not a native of Beijing, but I have on and off lived for forty years in Beijing. And during all these years, I have cemented a strong bound with the alleys and lanes in this city.

It is a long story that began in the summer of 1957. I was working as a statistician at a construction site in Kuijiachang Lane in the East District. Fascinated with paintings, at almost every noon break, I would go and see paintings by the master painter Xu Beihong at a museum dedicated to his memory at 16 East Shoulu Street nearby. I saw the same paintings repeatedly with continued interest. The museum was in a typical quadrangle house reigned by tranquility and elegance and grown with Chinese wisteria, persimmon trees, hollyhocks and magnolia trees. I enjoyed taking walks in the courtyard and sitting in the shade of Chinese toon trees after viewing the paintings. In the years to come, I visited former residences of such noted figures in the cultural field as Lu Xun, Mei Lanfang, Qi Baishi, Lao She and Mao Dun, all of which were in quadrangle houses. It seemed all the outstanding writers and artists loved the environment provided by quadrangle houses in lanes, leaving behind a residential culture in Beijing. A writer once said: "Without the lanes, modern literature in China would have been half significant than it has been." This is no exaggeration.

From 1959, I began a five-year study at the Central Academy of Fine Arts in Jiaoweiying Lane in the East District and became familiar with the alleys and lanes of various sizes in the vicinity. Most of my teachers lived in quadrangle houses on Shuaifu, Meizha and Dayabao lanes. To go into quadrangle houses when visiting my teachers thus became a routine.

The end of 1970s was no ordinary time for me as my wife Wang Changqing who had lived in another city for twelve years came with our two children to join me in Beijing. Our home was in Baiwanzhuang in the West District, but our work place was in Dengshikou in the East District. We rode our bikes to and from work and most of the time we avoided main streets and took the lanes. Riding in the turning and twisting lanes, it seemed our fatigue from the day's work disappeared. Though we later moved into an apartment building on Baishu Lane near Dengshikou, down below stood the straight lanes and neatly laid-out quadrangle houses. We loved to view the changes in the seasons and the life of the people in these houses. In the process we also took pictures when driven by inspiration.

Since 1980s, urban construction in the speed like a whirlwind has been sweeping through Beijing, resulting in daily changes in the physical appearance of the city. Yesterday's quadrangle houses on a lane are suddenly nowhere to be seen today. The familiar alleys and lanes of today may change completely tomorrow. On one of our interview trips to a residential area near Fuchengmen, we walked into a courtyard of quadrangle houses that were being torn down. In front of broken houses, stood an old man. His whole family had moved into an apartment building, but he could not help coming back to take one final look at his old house which would soon disappear completely and forever. He picked and took with him the final red ripening fruit on a Chinese wolfberry plant.

The culture of the lanes in the capital city has a splendid past, and crystallizes the wisdom and creativeness of the people. We felt at a loss as what to do in the quiet disappearing of the lanes along with a culture of a particular historic period. We realized there was an urgent need to record through the camera len the true features of the culture of lanes. We wanted to muster the little strength and resources we had to capture the historical footprints of the culture of lanes in this ancient capital city, the myriad vistas of people, their typical way of life and customs and habits unique to these lanes. Our contribution may not amount to much of a creative surprise. It was meant an attempt to rescue a cultural heritage, collecting data of images for people to do research and studies of a passing culture in the future. We found this a worthwhile job, though it was hard and cost a lot of time and sweat. In doing so, we were not going after monetary payment or an award of any kind, but simply driven by a sense of duty. That is all of our purpose.

To photograph the life of the ordinary people residing the alleys and lanes has taken virtually all of our spare-time. With the help of bicycles, we have visited every corner of the alleys and lanes, many of which we visited more than once. Each time we went to observe and photograph them under different conditions, we had new feelings and discoveries. Sometimes our target seemed entirely ordinary, but we still plucked up courage to find, and we were always successful in finding, fascinating vistas.

The quadrangle houses have nurtured generations of Beijingers. Having been the stage in the life of Beijing residents, they have seen the most fantastic merge and clash of modern life and traditional ways. When we ventured into crowded courtyards of simple living conditions, each providing home to several families, the residents poured out to us the difficulties of living in such an environment and their longing for moving into apartment buildings with modern facilities. We realized that the change in the traditional houses in the lanes was inevitable and irresistible. We tried to capture the true images of culture with our cameras with all our passion, in the hope that those who have lived in or are familiar with alleys and quadrangle houses in Beijing may find their own life or feelings and relive their past when reading this book.

May 1996
Forget-to-Return Study, Beijing

后 记

我是江南人,并非京城胡同里的土著。但前前后后在北京生活了四十年,与胡同和四合院结下了难解之缘。

说来话长,记得1957年的夏天,我在东城盔甲厂胡同的一个建筑工地上当统计员,业余迷恋绘画,每日午间休息时间差不多都要到临近的东受禄街16号的徐悲鸿纪念馆去看画。绘画大师的作品,尽管反复欣赏兴致亦未见稍减。纪念馆是个典型的四合院,方方正正,典雅宁静,院落里植着紫藤、柿树、蜀葵和玉兰,欣赏了作品再在院中走走,静坐在大椿树的绿荫里真是难得的从容、安详和惬意。以后的日子我又去过京城的鲁迅、梅兰芳、齐白石、老舍、茅盾故居,都是一座座四合院,文化巨匠和泰斗们喜爱居住在胡同四合院的空间环境里,由此留下了京城名人故居的宅邸文化。有位作家说:"没有胡同,中国现当代文学史塌了半边天。"此话不算过分。

1959年以后,我连续五年在东城校尉营胡同的中央美术学院求学。走熟了附近的大大小小胡同。老师们大部分居住在帅府胡同、煤渣胡同、大雅宝胡同的四合院里,所以拜访老师出入四合院更是常事。

七十年代不寻常,两地分居了十二年的内人王长青与两个孩子迁来京城,宿舍在西城百万庄,工作单位在东城灯市口,我俩常骑自行车上下班,十有八九喜欢躲开大街正道,从胡同里曲曲弯弯地赶路,一天工作的忙碌疲惫在穿行胡同中彷佛消融了许多。后来家又搬到了灯市东口的柏树胡同,虽然住的是楼房,但阳台下就是一条规规矩矩的胡同和一片四合院,对胡同里春夏秋冬、阴晴雨雪的景观和周围百姓的平凡生活,常有"相看两不厌"的感觉,兴致一来就拍摄一些照片。

八十年代以后,北京的城市建设似一场飓风席卷而来,京城的面貌发生着日新月异的变化。昨天存在的胡同四合院,今天突然消失了;今天熟悉的大街小巷,不久就是面目一新。记得有一次我俩到阜成门附近居民区采访,走进一片正在拆迁的四合院老房子之间,在已经拆毁的断墙残壁前站着一位老人。他的全家已经搬进了新建的公寓楼房,可他还是留恋不舍地来看看这些行将消失的老房子,摘走了老院子里最后一束红熟了的枸杞子。

京城胡同文化有过辉煌的过去,凝聚着前人的智慧和创造。我们深为胡同作为一个特定历史时代的文化的不辞而别而感到措手不及,胡同文化的面貌急待用摄影纪实的手法"留真"下来。尽我们微薄的力量留下一些古都胡同文化的历史陈迹,胡同天地里的百姓世相,京味京韵的民俗风情和市井氛围,虽算不上惊人的创作,却干了一点抢救遗产的活儿,为后来者追寻、研究即将逝去的胡同文化,留一点形象的资料。这是摄影力所能及的一种功能,作为从事摄影的苦力,流点汗水也是值得的,不求报酬,不图奖赏,责任感的驱使,仅此而已。

拍摄胡同和胡同里普通百姓的生活,多年来几乎占用了我俩所有的节假日休息时间。我们靠骑自行车走遍了古城的处处胡同旮旯,大部分胡同去了许多次,但在不同的条件下观察拍摄,总有一些新的感受与发现,有时对象平淡无奇,还须鼓足勇气去发掘那引人入胜的某些侧面。

胡同四合院曾经养育了一代又一代北京人,它是北京百姓生活的舞台。现代生活与传统文化的融汇与撞击在这里表现得淋漓尽致。当我们闯进那些人口拥挤、居住条件简陋的大杂院时,居民们会滔滔不绝地诉说居住在大杂院里的种种不便,盼望早早搬迁,住进有现代化生活设施的公寓之中,所以旧胡同四合院的变迁是势不可挡的了。我们虽是凭手中的照相机进行纪实留真,也少不了融进自己的感情。希望熟悉或曾在胡同四合院里生活过的人们,在阅读这本画册时,可以从中观照自己,追寻遗梦,产生共鸣。

沈延太
1996年5月于京城忘归斋

About the authors

Shen Yantai, born in Shanghai, 1939, graduated from Beijing Academy of Fine Arts in 1964. He used to work as an art editor and photographer for the *People's China* magazine. Participating in the first exploration of the origin of the Yangtze River in 1976, he became the first person to photograph the river from source to entry into the sea. Since 1980, he has served as judge of international photographic art exhibitions and national photographic contests. His works have been displayed at national and world photographic art shows and won several domestic and international awards. He has visited Britain, the United States, Japan, the former Soviet Union, Hong Kong and Macao for academic exchanges.

Covering a broad spectrum of subjects, his works present scenic sights, people and social customs. He is a frequent writer of photography reviews for newspapers and journals. His publications include a collection of pictures entitled *Images of Great Rivers*.

Shen now serves as deputy editor-in-chief of the English edition of *Women of China* monthly, council member of China Photographers Association, vice chairman of China Contemporary Photography Society, executive council member and vice director of Membership Evaluation Committee of the International Society of Chinese Photographers.

Wang Changqing was born in Taiyuan City, Shanxi Province, 1945 and graduated from Shanxi University in 1968. She is now a reporter and editor of *Women of China* magazine, member of China Photographers Association, China Women Photographers Association, Beijing Association of Women Journalists and Beijing Association of Photographers. She was listed in *China Photographers Directory* in 1987.

Wang is particularly good at photographing the life of women and children and often writes feature stories supported with pictures on this subject. Her works have been exhibited both in China and abroad and awarded prizes at national photography exhibitions and competitions.

作者简介

沈延太,1939年生于上海,1964年毕业于北京中央美术学院,同年任《人民中国》杂志社美术编辑、摄影记者。现任英文《中国妇女》杂志社副总编辑、编审,中国摄影家协会理事,中国当代摄影学会副主席,世界华人摄影学会执行委员、会员评审委员会副主任。

1976年曾参加长江源头首次探险考察,只身完成了长江全程摄影报道,成为"长江全程摄影第一人"。1980年以来多次担任国际摄影艺术展览及各类全国性摄影比赛评委。其摄影作品在国家及国际摄影艺术展览和名家联展中,多次荣获国内、国际大奖。作品题材广泛,尤以风光、风情、人物见长。

曾往英、美、日、原苏联等国及香港、澳门地区进行学术交流。其摄影理论著述时见于报刊,曾出版专集《大江影踪》等。

王长青,女,1945年生于山西省太原市,1968年毕业于山西大学。现任《中国妇女》杂志社记者、编辑,为中国摄影家协会、中国女摄影家协会、北京市女新闻工作者协会、北京市摄影家协会会员。1987年被载入《中国摄影家大辞典》。

擅长拍摄妇女儿童生活题材,常以图文并茂的形式进行专题报导。作品多次参与国内外展出,曾在全国性影展、影赛中获奖。

图书在版编目(CIP)数据

京城胡同留真:英汉对照/沈延太编;王长青,沈延太摄影.
—北京:外文出版社,1997
ISBN 7-119-01917-1

Ⅰ.北… Ⅱ.①沈… ②王… ③沈… Ⅲ.居住建筑-北京
-摄影集-英、汉 Ⅳ.TU-881.2

中国版本图书馆 CIP 数据核字 (97) 第 05015 号

京城胡同留真

沈延太 编

*

ⓒ 外文出版社

外文出版社出版
(中国北京百万庄大街24号)
邮政编码100037
深圳兴裕印刷制版有限公司制版
深圳当纳利旭日印刷有限公司印刷
中国国际图书贸易总公司发行
(中国北京车公庄西路35号)
北京邮政信箱第399号 邮政编码100044
1997年(12开)第1版
(英汉)
ISBN 7-119-01917-1 /J·1383(外)
12800
85-EC-479S